THE HANDBOOK OF
THE WEATHER

THE HANDBOOK OF
THE WEATHER

GERRIE McCALL

This edition first published in 2003 for Grange Books
An imprint of Grange Books plc
The Grange
Kingsnorth Industrial Estate
Hoo, nr Rochester
Kent ME3 9ND
www.grangebooks.co.uk

ISBN: 1-84013-594-8

Editorial and Design by:
Amber Books Ltd
Bradley's Close
74–77 White Lion Street
London N1 9PF
www.amberbooks.co.uk

Project Editor: Mariano Kälfors/Charlotte Berman
Design: Hawes Design
Illustrations: Tony Randell and Kevin Jones Associates

PICTURE CREDITS
Front cover: Corbis
Artworks: Amber Books Ltd/Tony Randell

Publisher's note
Neither the author nor the publishers can accept any responsibility for any
loss, injury or damage, caused as a result of the use of techniques described
in this book. Nor for any prosecutions or proceedings brought or instigated
against any person or body that may result from using these techniques.

Printed in Italy by Eurolitho S.p.A.

Contents

Introduction

We tend to take the weather for granted until it shows its violent side. Flooding, extremes in temperature, hurricanes, tornadoes and thunderstorms demonstrate our weather system's awesome power.

The focus of this book is to help you be better prepared for extreme weather conditions when your survival is at stake.

The very essence of survival is confronting and conquering a set of challenges. Extreme weather presents challenges to both your health and property. Advance planning for dangerous weather is a vital element for survival. Techniques for safeguarding your home, finding water, building fires and shelters, dressing to protect yourself, driving in snow, assembling survival kits, avoiding heat- and cold-related illnesses and signaling for help are some of the practical skills outlined in this book.

Learning to identify weather phenomena is an important step to preparedness. With that in mind, this book begins with an overview of the world's weather that explains the atmospheric forces that interact to create our weather. Modern forecasting methods are also explained, and with this basic information about world weather patterns, winds and pressure systems, you can command a greater understanding of what the weather might do next and identify the onset of potentially dangerous weather.

Past survivors of hurricanes, floods, tornadoes, and extreme temperatures have not necessarily been trained in survival techniques. Those who have survived kept a positive mindset, remained calm, and possessed an overwhelming desire to live. The combination of a determined, positive outlook and basic preparedness are essential qualities of a survivor.

By reading this book, you are taking the first step in preparedness. Even if an extreme weather event takes you by surprise, having this information will give you an understanding of what steps need to be taken to ensure everyone's safety. Those who remain calm and have a plan of action are natural leaders in a survival situation.

Your natural tenacity and optimism combined with the methods outlined in this book will provide you with the skills you need to survive the weather in all its forms.

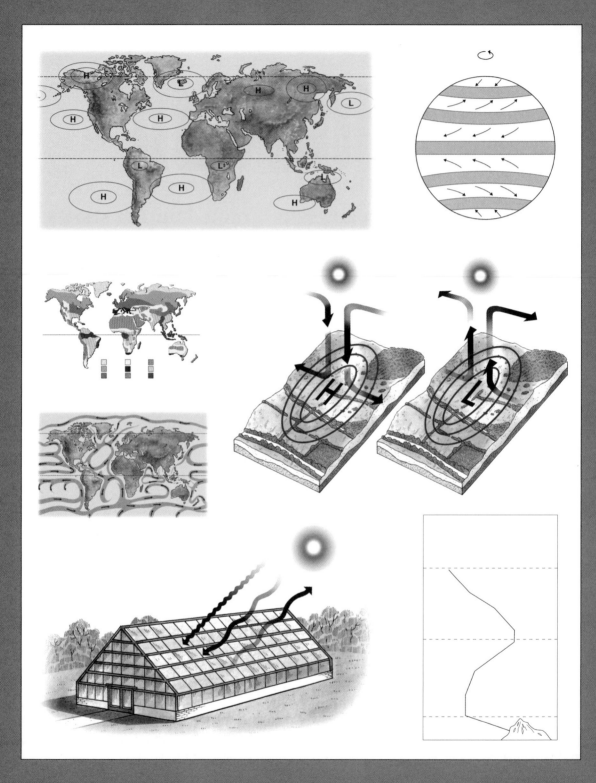

CHAPTER ONE

The World's Weather

The weather influences everything we do, from deciding which clothes to wear, to the types of homes we build, the food we eat and the sports we enjoy. There is no avoiding the weather. However, the answer to coping with extreme weather conditions and events lies in understanding and preparation.

The complex interactions between the atmosphere, the rotation of earth, ocean currents, climate, global wind currents and the sun create our weather. A basic understanding of these weather-influencing elements can help you anticipate your area's susceptibility to various kinds of extreme weather. Knowing what sort of weather to anticipate allows you to prepare for it and survive potentially deadly situations.

WEATHER VERSUS CLIMATE

The term weather is used to describe short-term variations in the atmosphere around us. Daily reports on temperature, precipitation and cloud cover issued by meteorologists in their forecasts describe the local weather.

Climate, on the other hand, describes the average of day-to-day weather conditions over an extended period of time. Daily weather observations stretching back at least 30 years are assembled to determine an area's climatic patterns. These observations include measurements of minimum and maximum daily temperatures and average monthly rainfall.

EARTH'S ATMOSPHERE

Earth is surrounded by the atmosphere – a thin blanket of different types of gas. Without the atmosphere, life could not exist on earth. It protects us from meteors and filters the sun's intense radiation and also provides the oxygen we need to breathe. The driving force behind earth's weather phenomena is the interaction between the sun and the atmosphere. The sun heating our atmosphere leads to the formation and circulation of air masses. Circulating air masses cause air pressure differences which give us either fair or stormy weather.

Atmospheric layers

The atmosphere's layers are delineated according to their temperature profiles. Hot-air balloonists in the 19th century discovered that the temperature of the atmosphere decreased as they ascended. This observation holds true for approximately 9.65km (6 miles) upwards throughout the troposphere. In 1899, a French meteorologist named Leon Teisserenc de Bort reported his discovery that the temperature ceased to drop at an altitude of about 9.65km (6 miles) where a new layer of atmosphere began.

Troposphere: where 99 per cent of our weather occurs. It extends 0–10km (0–6 miles) above earth's surface and contains the air we breathe. The average drop in temperature is 7°C per km (4°F per 1000 ft) as you ascend. At the tropopause, where the troposphere ceases, temperatures can be as low as -58°C (-70°F). Virtually all of the clouds, precipitation and water vapour are found here.

Stratosphere: where the ozone layer is, 24km (15 miles) high. The entire stratosphere extends 10–50km (6–30 miles) above earth's surface. Temperatures in the stratosphere slowly increase to about 4°C (40°F) as you ascend.

Mesosphere: extends 50–80km (30–50 miles) above earth's surface. Here temperatures begin to decrease again, dropping to about -90°C (-130°F) at the mesopause, or the top of the mesosphere.

Thermosphere: protects us from meteors and decommissioned satellites by burning them up before they can reach earth. Here temperatures rise dramatically to as much as 1650°C (3000°F). Also known as the ionosphere, it extends 80–500 km (50–310 miles) above earth's surface.

Exosphere: location where satellites orbit. Temperatures can range anywhere from 300°C (570°F) to 1650°C (3000°F). This layer begins approximately 500km (310 miles) above earth's surface and blends into interplanetary space.

WORLD CLIMATIC ZONES

When determining climatic zones, rainfall patterns, sea-surface temperatures, vegetation zones, wind patterns and average air temperatures are all taken into account. Long-term observations – over several decades – rather than seasonal observations are used to delineate climate.

Tropical: occurs primarily between the Tropic of Cancer and Tropic of Capricorn. Characterized by high rainfall, high humidity, high temperatures and a brief dry season. Singapore has a tropical climate.

Subtropical: characterized by wet and dry seasons of almost equal lengths and a broader temperature range than found in tropical climates. Calcutta, India has a subtropical climate.

Arid: characterized by extreme daily and seasonal temperature fluctuations and very little rainfall. Extremely low humidity allows most of the sun's radiation to reach the ground. Summer daytime temperatures can reach as high as 49°C (120°F). Alice Springs, Australia has an arid climate.

Predominant surface winds

There are three predominant wind systems at the earth's surface, named after the direction from which they originate. These are the Hadley cells or trade winds, which are easterly winds near the equator, the westerly mid-latitude Ferrell cells, and the polar easterlies.

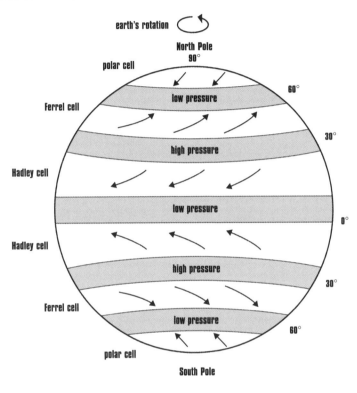

Semi-arid: large expanses of grassland and more rainfall and less extreme seasonal temperature fluctuations. Johannesburg, South Africa has a semi-arid climate.

Mediterranean: mild, moist winters and dry, sunny summers influenced by proximity to oceans. Little rainfall for four to six months of the year. Milan, Italy has a Mediterranean climate.

Coastal: temperatures influenced by the moderating effects of the ocean. Less extreme temperatures than inland areas. Rio de Janeiro, Brazil has a coastal climate.

Temperate: four distinct seasons with uniform rainfall. Characterised by warm, humid summers and cold, snowy winters. Glasgow, Scotland has a temperate climate.

Northern Temperate: similar to temperate climate with longer, harsher winters that last up to nine months. Has permafrost, an underlying layer of permanently frozen soil. Sakhalin Island, Russia is one example.

Mountain: higher altitude makes this climate cooler than lower-lying climates at the same latitude. Mountain climates are windy and they experience regular snowfalls. Kathmandu, Nepal is an example of a typical mountain climate.

Polar: found at the north and south poles, Polar regions have very little rainfall and experience frequent snowfall. Extremely long, cold winter months characterize this climate. Six months of continuous summer daylight are followed by six months of non-stop winter darkness. Barrow, Alaska has a polar climate.

LANDMASSES AND WEATHER

Large landmasses can affect temperature, precipitation and pressure systems. The atmosphere's interaction with landmasses produces the clouds and storms of local weather. It also affects the temperature range and average rainfall that are measures of climatic patterns.

When an air mass encounters a barrier, such as a mountain, it will rise. The rising air condenses, clouds form and precipitation falls. Moist sea breezes blowing over sun-heated land rise and condense, resulting in rain. When a hurricane makes landfall, it slows and soon dies out because it is no

Predominant pressure centers in January

There are five semi-permanent high-pressure cells referred to as the subtropical highs. These highs remain over the ocean basins throughout the year because temperatures and pressures there tend to remain constant. This is where the highs and lows are located in January, which is winter in the Northern Hemisphere.

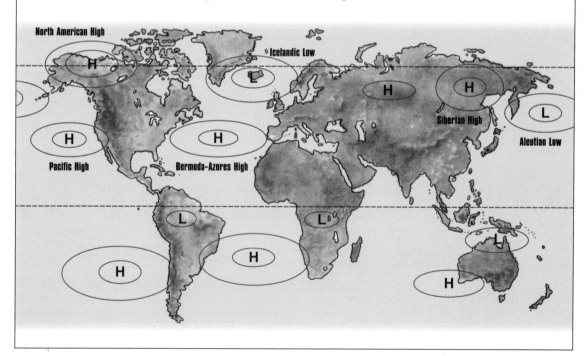

longer fed by the ocean's warm water. Semi-permanent high- and low-pressure areas form over inland continental regions as a result of interaction between air and land temperatures. The effect of landmasses is just one variable in the behaviour of weather.

GLOBAL WINDS

The sun strikes different parts of earth with varying intensities. The resulting variations in temperature give rise to diverse patterns of airflow. Recognized global wind patterns are the result of these circulating patterns of airflow. Weather at different locations on the globe is directly affected by these wind pat-

terns. The three major vertical circulations of air in each hemisphere are the Hadley cell, the Ferrell cell and the polar cell.

Hadley cells: adjacent to the equator, extending from 0° to 30° north and south. The sun causes warm humid air, near the equator in the tropics, to rise and form clouds and thunderstorms. When the rising air reaches the tropopause, it cools down, spreads and sinks again creating a high-pressure area. A portion of this air moves again towards the low-pressure area near the equator. These are known as the northeast trade winds in the Northern Hemisphere

Predominant pressure centers in July

The pressure centers shift with changing seasonal temperatures during the Northern Hemisphere's summer months. The shift is more pronounced over the continents because

land areas heat and cool more drastically than the oceans. The change in temperatures effect changes in pressure. This is where the highs and lows are located during the summer.

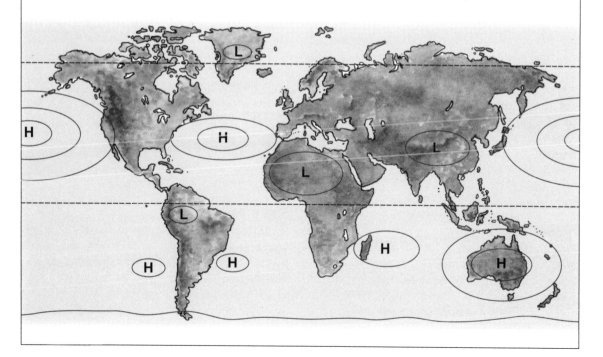

and the southeast trade winds in the Southern Hemisphere.

Ferrell cells: lie between 30° and 60° north and south. Most of the sinking air that descends near 30° north and south continues as part of the Hadley cell, but some of this air circulates towards the poles until it encounters colder polar air near 60° north and south.

Polar cells: occur from 60° north and south to the poles. Frigid polar air sinks and flows away from the poles until it meets the Ferrell cells. This air is warmed and circulated back towards the poles. Because these cold, dry winds generally move from east to west, they are also referred to as polar easterlies.

Doldrums: are found where the trade winds from both hemispheres meet near the equator. Also called the Intertropical Convergence Zone (ITCZ). Converging winds die out here because ocean-warmed air rises in this area.

Jet Streams: two fast-moving streams of air that occur in the upper part of the troposphere. Jet streams are caused by temperature and pressure changes, following the boundaries between cold and hot air. The polar-front jet follows the boundary of the Ferrell and polar cells. The subtropical jet follows the boundary of the Hadley and Ferrell cells. Their general direction is westerly, but they can veer northwards and southwards.

FRONTAL SYSTEMS

The Bergen School, a team of Norwegian meteorologists that worked together immediately after World War I, gave the world the concept of fronts. Named after the World War I battle fronts where soldiers fought, a weather front is found where air masses with differing temperatures clash.

Air masses

A body of air made up of relatively constant temperature and humidity is an air mass. An air mass can measure from a few square kilometres (miles) in size to thousands of square kilometres (miles). Air masses are moved around by global winds.

It is the interaction of different air masses that creates weather. The leading edges, or boundaries, between air masses with different temperatures are called fronts.

Warm fronts

When a mass of warm air moves into an area with colder air, it is called a warm front. The warmer air rises over the retreating mass of cold air. As the warm air rises, it cools and condenses. The result is stratus clouds and precipitation over a wide area.

Cold fronts

When a mass of cold air moves into an area with warmer air it is called a cold front. Cold fronts move more quickly than warm fronts and produce sudden changes in local weather. The less dense warm air is forced upwards suddenly by the advancing cold air. Warm air will always rise above cold air despite which front is advancing. The rapid rising of warm air, caused by the arrival of a cold front, forms cumulus clouds that can produce thunderstorms and heavy precipitation.

PRESSURE SYSTEMS

High and low pressure areas play a key role in determining weather events.

High pressure

A high-pressure system consists of cool, sinking air that rotates clockwise when found in the Northern Hemisphere. In the Southern Hemisphere it rotates anti-clockwise (counterclockwise). As the air sinks, it warms and spreads out. The sinking air slows down the formation of clouds, so high-pressure systems are normally

Formation of high and low pressure areas

As air cools and sinks, high pressure areas form. As warm air rises, cools, and spreads, low pressure areas form. The rising air associated with low pressure areas often results in cloud formation. The sinking air from high pressure areas feeds into areas of low pressure. The air movement from areas of high to low pressure is known as wind.

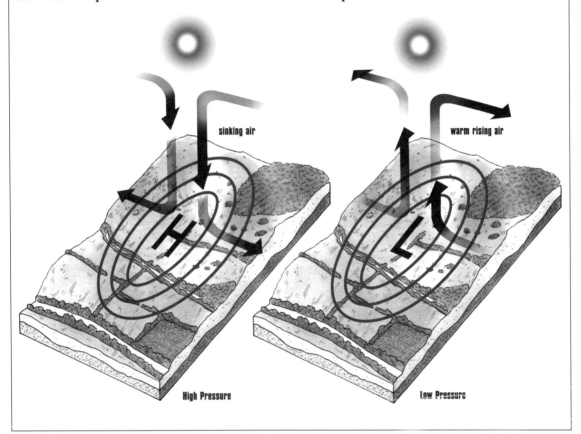

sinking air

warm rising air

High Pressure

Low Pressure

associated with fair weather. These systems are also referred to as anticyclones.

Low pressure

A low-pressure system consists of warm, rising air that rotates anti-clockwise (counterclockwise) when found in the Northern Hemisphere. In the Southern Hemisphere it rotates clockwise. This air cools down and spreads out as it rises. The rising air produces clouds and thunderstorms, but they tend to cover a smaller area than high-pressure systems. These systems are also referred to as cyclones.

OCEAN CURRENTS

There is a direct link between weather and oceans. The oceans cover about 70 per cent of earth's surface and contain 97 per cent of earth's water. Water that has evaporated from the oceans accounts for almost 90 per cent of the precipitation that falls on land.

Fluctuation of average global temperatures

By studying ice core samples drilled in Greenland, scientists can determine the history of Earth's average temperature. The age of the ice can be calculated from its depth within the core. Elements within the core sample reveal how cold the climate was at the time the ice formed. These ice cores reveal that large-scale cooling occurs approximately every 180 years.

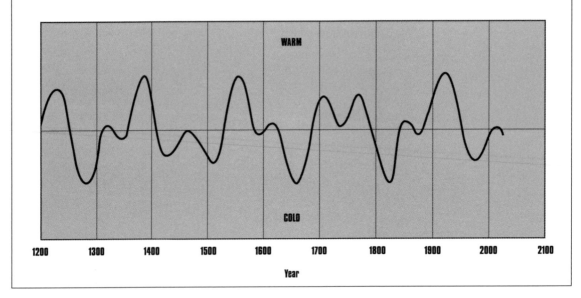

The principal ocean currents are influenced by global wind patterns. These currents circulate warm and cold water around the earth. The temperatures of these currents affect the temperature at the surface of the sea, which in turn affects the climate of landmasses. A good example of this is the effect the Gulf Stream has on Great Britain. The warming effects of the Gulf Stream give Great Britain milder winters than those experienced by countries located at similar latitudes but farther inland away from the Gulf Stream's influence.

Winds from mid-latitude high-pressure systems drive ocean currents that move clockwise in the Northern Hemisphere and anti-clockwise (counterclockwise) in the Southern Hemisphere. The ocean's major cold currents tend to reduce rainfall over coastal land. This is because the cool air above the current is generally too dry to lead to cloud formation. The ocean's major warm currents produce warmer temperatures over adjacent coastal lands. The changes these warm currents cause in sea-surface temperatures tend to spawn low-pressure centres, which result in high winds and heavy rain over coastal areas.

El Niño

The occurrence of El Niño has been documented since 1726, but it did not gain international attention until the catastrophic events of 1982–3. El Niño events occur on average every three to eight years and can last for up to three years. It is a warm current that arrives off the western coast of South America near Ecuador and Peru in late

December. Because it arrives close to Christmas, it was given the Spanish name El Niño in honour of the infant Jesus.

El Niño causes a shift in where the largest thunderstorms occur over the Pacific. Weather patterns are affected because the thunderstorms disturb the upper air in different places more than usual and normal high- and low-pressure areas and wind patterns are shifted. The 1982–3 El Niño triggered a number of events including widespread flooding in Peru and Ecuador; severe droughts in Australia, Indonesia, the Philippines, India, Mexico and Southern Africa; multiple tropical storms in French Polynesia after a 75-year-long period in which none had occurred; and severe storms on the west coast of the United States.

Weather events associated with El Niño have led many to believe that earth is experiencing an increasing pattern of natural disasters. Overall, however, world weather events are not changing in terms of frequency or intensity. What has changed is a heightened awareness of extreme weather events through improved forecasting and reporting methods. An increase in the world's population makes it inevitable that more people's lives are affected by extreme weather inevitable.

GLOBAL TEMPERATURE CHANGES

There is a lot of debate in the scientific

Greenhouse effect

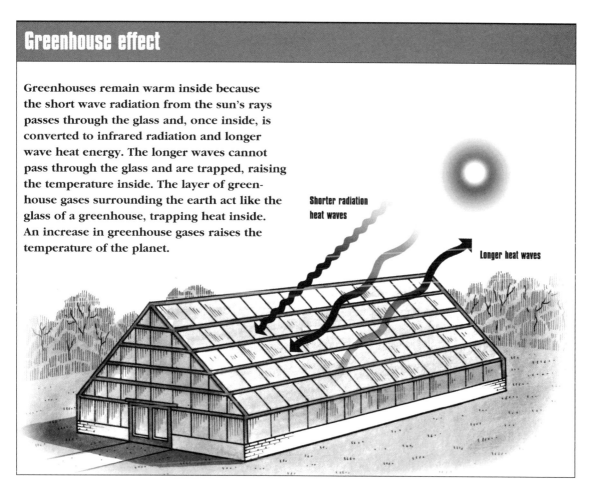

Greenhouses remain warm inside because the short wave radiation from the sun's rays passes through the glass and, once inside, is converted to infrared radiation and longer wave heat energy. The longer waves cannot pass through the glass and are trapped, raising the temperature inside. The layer of greenhouse gases surrounding the earth act like the glass of a greenhouse, trapping heat inside. An increase in greenhouse gases raises the temperature of the planet.

Shorter radiation heat waves

Longer heat waves

community about climate change. Some scientists are certain that earth's temperature is cooling; they believe that the earth is approaching another ice age. Others cite evidence of global warming as an indicator that the greenhouse effect is causing earth's temperature to rise dangerously. The truth is, earth's climate has always undergone change. Global temperature naturally tends to fluctuate over long periods of time.

Ice core samples drilled by scientists in Greenland revealed much about the history of earth's climate because air trapped in the ice reveals the composition of past atmosphere. Past precipitation levels are determined by examining the thickness of annual ice layers, and chemical analysis determines at what temperature the precipitation occurred. Analysis of ice core samples demonstrated a tendency for cooling to take place approximately every 180 years. Likewise, tree rings, coral, ocean beds and the sediment in lakes have also been examined for clues about earth's fluctuating temperature.

Map of world climates

The global classification of climate zones is based on maximum and minimum temperatures, the temperature range and the total and seasonal distribution of precipitation. The factors that affect climate are: distance from the equator (latitude), altitude, winds, distance from the sea (continentality), and whether or not the slopes face the sun (aspect).

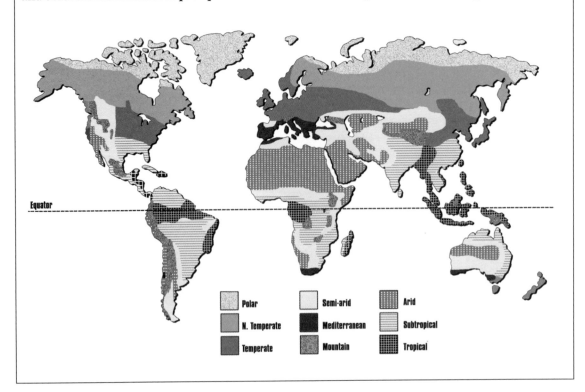

Equator

☐ Polar		☐ Semi-arid		▦ Arid	
▨ N. Temperate		■ Mediterranean		▤ Subtropical	
▨ Temperate		▨ Mountain		▦ Tropical	

Principal ocean currents

Prevailing winds from high pressure systems in the mid-latitudes move currents that circulate clockwise in the Northern Hemisphere and counterclockwise in the Southern Hemisphere. These currents transport warm or cool water great distances and influence the climate of landmasses. Generally the currents near the poles are coldest and currents near the equator are warmest.

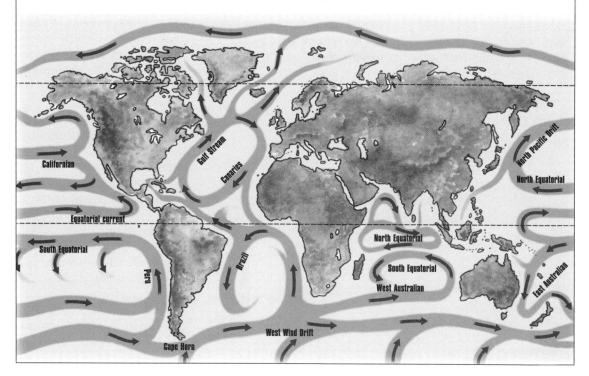

Factors affecting climate change

There are numerous factors that can affect a shift in climate. The amount of sun reaching earth is the most important astronomical force in determining climate. In the 1930s, Milutin Milankovitch, a Yugoslav geophysicist, proposed a theory that links long-term climate change with variations in earth's orbit. He cited slow changes in earth's orbit and shifts in the tilt of its axis as factors affecting its position in relation to the sun. The Milankovitch theory explains alterations in the amount of sunlight falling on earth at different latitudes.

Volcanic eruptions can also affect earth's temperature and spark global weather changes. Dust particles and gases ejected by the eruptions can be spread round the world by stratospheric winds. This material blocks the amount of sun that reaches earth's surface and causes short-term temperature changes.

A peak in sunspot activity every 11 years has been linked to patterns of warm and cool weather. Another theory connects the orbit of our solar system through dust lanes to the occurrence of ice ages every 150 million years. The fact is, there are numerous, naturally occurring phenomena that can trigger either long- or short-term shifts in earth's temperature.

Layers of the atmosphere

The four layers of the earth's atmosphere are defined by their temperature profiles. Though all layers have some effect on the earth's climate, 99% of our weather occurs in the lowest of the layers, the troposphere.

Ozone destruction

The ozone layer is located in the stratosphere. It absorbs most of the sun's damaging ultra-violet rays and helps prevent some heat loss from earth. A hole in the ozone layer, which is more accurately described as an area of severely depleted ozone, was discovered over Antarctica. While the amount of ozone over the poles naturally fluctuates, scientists believe that human activities have contributed to its rapid depletion. Especially damaging to the ozone are chlorofluorocarbons (CFCs). Until the mid-1990s, CFCs were widely used as propellants in aerosol cans, as well as in refrigeration, air-conditioning systems and fire extinguishers. CFCs form chlorine compounds in the upper atmosphere, which destroy ozone. In reaction to this threat, countries around the world are replacing CFCs with chemicals that are not as great a threat to the ozone layer.

Greenhouse effect

Greenhouse gases that occur naturally keep earth at a temperature that makes it habitable for humans by controlling how much heat is radiated away from earth. These gases only pose a problem when human activities increase them to the point where too much heat is retained in our atmosphere. The burning of fossil fuels aggravates the greenhouse effect by adding to the concentration of carbon dioxide, methane, CFCs and nitrous oxide. These additional greenhouse gases radiate too much heat back towards earth, changing the climate.

Global warming

In the past 100 years, the global climate has warmed by about 0.5°C (1°F). It is difficult to determine how much of this warming is a result of human influences versus natural processes. While the burning of fossil fuels aggravates the greenhouse effect and contributes to global warming, so do natural changes in the environment. Air temperature is only one factor in climatic change. El Niño's effect on rainfall patterns is now widely considered to be the culprit for the drought and desert expansion of the 1970s. It is important to remember that there are many interrelated factors that affect the climate and it is difficult to determine whether our planet is cooling or warming at this point without the benefit of objective hindsight. Every argument that the global temperature is changing in one direction can be met with a counter-argument that it is changing in the opposite direction. Only with the benefit of years of climatic observations as evidence will our great-grandchildren be able to make an accurate assessment of which direction our current global temperature is heading. The complex combination of factors that influence our climate's delicate balance has long been the subject of meteorologists' increasingly sophisticated predictions.

CHAPTER TWO

Predicting the Weather

Methods of predicting the weather have been transformed by technological advances. Weather forecasting has evolved from primitive guesses based on observations of plant and animal behavior to a worldwide cooperative network of scientists using highly accurate satellite images, radar and computer modeling.

On 7 September 1900, residents of Galveston, Texas gathered along the shore to watch the unusually high waves. Isaac Cline, the head of the local weather bureau, had been watching his barometer readings drop steadily. Concerned about the potentially hazardous weather condition that he felt was imminent, Cline raised the hurricane warning flags, but the crowds continued to gather on the sunny beach. He mounted his horse and rode up and down the beach, warning everyone to take cover, but he was ignored. It was, after all, a beautiful day. Twenty-four hours later more than 6000 were dead.

Fortunately, methods used to forecast weather and disseminate storm warnings have vastly improved in the past 100 years. Current weather forecasting methods provide enough advance data about the strength and path of storms to allow time for evacuation. Modern meteorologists combine observations, radar, satellite photos and computer models to provide more accurate predictions. In 1992, Hurricane Andrew struck the Florida coast with forces equal to the storm of 1900 that hit Galveston. However, because ample warning of the approaching storm allowed time for people to evacuate, only 23 deaths were associated with Andrew.

NATURAL METHODS OF FORECASTING

Long before meteorologists on television and radio provided daily forecasts, people looked to signs in nature to predict the weather. Popular weather lore holds that animal behaviour can predict storms. Ants have been observed to build up earth round the entrance hole to their colony when rain approaches as a way to keep water from flooding their nest. Bees flying back to their hives and cows lying down in pastures are also believed to portend coming rains.

Plants too have long been regarded as harbingers of storms. Pine cones respond to increases in humidity levels by closing their scales, so a closed pine cone means wet weather and a pine cone with open scales indicates dry weather. Many other plants, including clover, shamrocks, morning glories and chicory, close their petals or leaves in response to increased humidity levels. When the silver maple tree turns up its leaves, rain is expected. The increased atmospheric pressure associated with the approach of a storm causes plants to open their pores and emit a stronger scent.

There are many factors other than approaching storms, however, that can affect the reaction of animals and plants to their environment. This renders plants and animals undependable weather forecasters.

Clouds

A more dependable method of forecasting from nature is observing what types of clouds are present. Because they consist of masses of condensing water vapour, their size and formation can offer clues about air pressure and temperature. As a rule of thumb, low dark clouds massed together indicate storms, whereas high white clouds indicate clear weather.

Clouds are generally given compound names based on their shape and height. The basic shapes are:

- *cumulus* – fluffy or heaped up
- *cirrus* – fibrous or curly
- *stratus* – layered or stratified

Prefixes are attached to indicate the height of the cloud:

- *cirro* is associated with the highest clouds with bases starting at about 7000m (20,000ft)
- *alto* is associated with mid-level clouds with bases starting between 1830 and 7000m (6000 and 20,000ft)
- *nimbo* is associated with a cloud producing precipitation (nimbus is the suffix form)

If you can recognize certain cloud formations, you can make an educated guess about the weather to come:

Cumulus: appear as fluffy white clouds. Cumulus is Latin for 'heap'. These clouds look like they are made of cotton wool but are flat along the bottom. These fair-weather clouds can indicate the passage of a warm front. However, if they enlarge and push upwards into the atmosphere, forming a mountain of clouds, they can form storm clouds.

Cumulonimbus: the result of a build-up of cumulus clouds. They tower to great heights and have an anvil formation at the top. Also called a 'thunderhead', these clouds bring thunderstorms. In colder temperatures, they can bring hail or snow.

Nimbus: a uniformly grey rain cloud that stretches across the entire sky.

Cirrus: very high clouds that form as thin streaks or curls. They normally indicate fair weather. In colder climates, when these clouds multiply and northerly winds blow steadily, a blizzard may be expected.

Types of cloud

Clouds are formed by arge masses of condensing water vapour. They are classified based on their altitude and shape. Fair-weather clouds tend to be higher and white. Low, black clouds clustered together indicate imminent storms. Many rain-producing cumulonimbus clouds can reach the top of the troposphere.

A. Cirrus
B. Cirrocumulus
C. Cirrostratus
D. Altocumulus
E. Altostratus
F. Stratocumulus
G. Nimbostratus
H. Cumulus
I. Stratus
J. Anvil Head
K. Cumulonimbus
L. Rain, hail and squall winds

Stratus: these clouds generally indicate rain. They are very low grey clouds that can either form a layer across the sky or appear in isolated tufts.

Cirrostratus: indicates fair weather. They appear as a thin white veil of clouds occurring as extensive layered streamers across the sky.

Cirrocumulus: a cirrus cloud with a texture, it has a patterned appearance, earning it the nickname 'mackerel sky'. This is a somewhat rare cloud formation caused by atmospheric instability, and can signal the approach of cold-front storms.

Meteorologists attach a series of Latin terms to clouds to further describe them:

castellanus – turret-shaped
congestus – swollen or developing
fibratus – formed in strands
humilis – humble or small
lenticularis – lens-shaped
mediocris – average- or medium-sized
uncinus – hooked
undulatus – formed in waves

MEASURING THE WEATHER

Since the 17th century meteorologists have used different tools to measure air temperature, air pressure, humidity and wind speed. Modern meteorologists have added computers, radar and satellites to their forecasting arsenal.

Humidity

Relative humidity depends upon the amount of water vapour in the air and the air's temperature. It is actually a measure of the water vapour present in the air compared to the amount of water vapour needed to saturate the air at that temperature. A comparison of a dry bulb thermometer reading and a wet bulb thermometer reading is used to determine relative humidity. The dry bulb thermometer measures the actual air temperature. The wet bulb thermometer has a damp muslin bag covering its bulb and measures the water vapour-saturated air. The difference in measurements between the two thermometers yields a percentage that describes relative humidity. If both thermometers show the same temperature, the relative humidity is 100 percent.

Air pressure

Barometers measure air pressure. Changes in air pressure indicate a change in weather. High pressure brings clear skies and fair weather. Low pressure brings wet and stormy weather. Both the mercury barometer and the aneroid barograph are used to make measurements of air pressure.

Mercury barometer

A mercury barometer measures air pressure in inches of mercury. A tube, sealed at one

Pine cones

Pine cones' reaction to humidity can be used as a natural predictor of weather. The humidity preceding wet weather allows the cone to absorb moisture and maintain its natural shape. In dry weather, the pine cone opens its scales.

Wet weather

Dry weather

Plant reactions to humidity

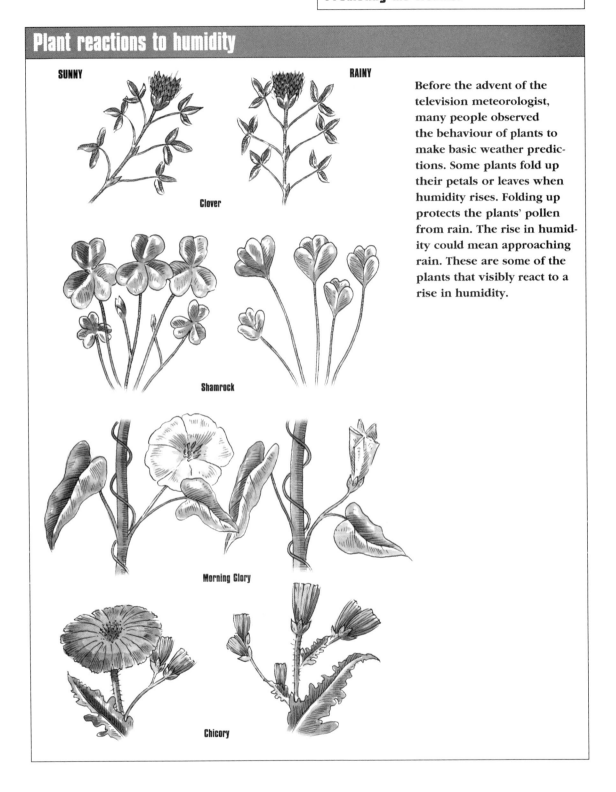

SUNNY

RAINY

Clover

Shamrock

Morning Glory

Chicory

Before the advent of the television meteorologist, many people observed the behaviour of plants to make basic weather predictions. Some plants fold up their petals or leaves when humidity rises. Folding up protects the plants' pollen from rain. The rise in humidity could mean approaching rain. These are some of the plants that visibly react to a rise in humidity.

Barograph

A barograph can record pressure changes over a week's time. The aneroid, a flexible metal bellow, is squeezed as pressure increases. It expands as pressure decreases. A lever transfers the aneroid's movement to a pen. The pen moves up and down as pressure changes, tracing a line on the paper that is mounted on a slowly revolving cylinder.

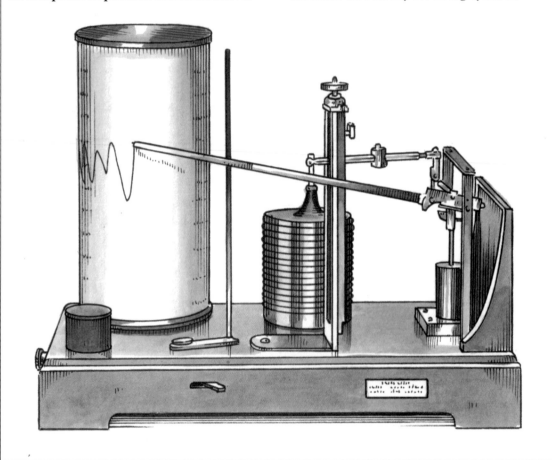

end, is partially filled with mercury and placed, open end down, in a container of mercury. Next to the tube is a ruler marked with inches. Air pressure bearing down on the mercury in the dish prevents the mercury in the tube from running out. Higher air pressure against the mercury in the dish forces the mercury up higher in the tube. Lower air pressure against the mercury in the dish allows the mercury in the tube to drop.

Aneroid barograph

In an aneroid barograph, expansion or contraction of a vacuum cylinder, or aneroid, is measured. As air pressure increases, the aneroid is squeezed. As air pressure decreases, the aneroid expands. The up and

The Beaufort Scale

Beaufort Number	Speed (mph)	Speed (kph)	Description	Effects on land
0	< 1	< 1	calm	calm; smoke rises vertically
1	2–3	1–5	light air	smoke drift indicates wind direction; vanes do not move
2	4–7	6–11	light breeze	wind felt on face; leaves rustle; vanes begin to move
3	8–12	12–19	gentle breeze	leaves, small twigs in constant motion; light flags extended
4	13–18	20–29	moderate breeze	dust, leaves and loose paper raised up; small branches move
5	19–24	30–38	fresh breeze	small trees in leaf begin to sway
6	25–31	39–51	strong breeze	large branches of trees in motion; whistling heard in utility wires
7	32–38	52–61	near gale	whole trees in motion; resistance felt in walking against wind
8	39–46	62–74	gale	twigs and small branches broken off trees
9	47–54	75–86	strong gale	slight structural damage occurs; slate blown from roofs
10	55–63	87–101	whole gale	seldom experienced on land; trees broken; structural damage occurs
11	64–74	102–120	storm	very rarely experienced on land; usually with widespread damage
12	> 74	> 120	hurricane force	violent; widespread destruction

down movement of the aneroid is transferred by levers to a pen. The pen records these fluctuations by drawing a line on paper attached to a slowly rotating cylinder. The paper on a single cylinder can record pressure changes for an entire week.

Weather stations

There are thousands of weather stations across the world where, every three hours, observers take measurements of the atmosphere and report them to weather bureaux. The instruments used in a weather station include thermometers and barometers. A pluviograph records how much rain falls over what time, and records these observations on a sheet of paper. An anemometer, which measures wind speed and direction, is

also used. For those civilian weather observers without an anemometer, the Beaufort Scale is used to establish wind speed based on general indicators.

Automatic weather stations

Automatic weather stations consist of ground-based equipment that automatically take readings of barometric pressure, humidity and temperature, along with the speed and direction of the wind. These observations are continuously transmitted automatically to weather services for use in forecasting.

Weather balloons

To measure conditions in the upper atmosphere, radiosondes are sent up via weather

Station model

A station model is used to plot synoptic weather data for weather maps. A station model provides a snapshot of an area's surface weather.

A system of symbols is used to indicate temperature, humidity, pressure, wind speed and direction, cloud amount and type, and visibility.

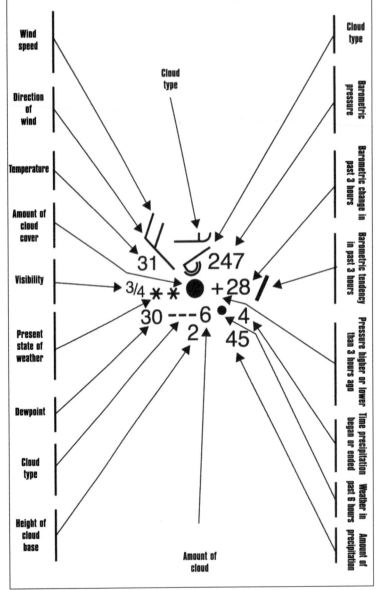

Wind speed

Direction of wind

Temperature

Amount of cloud cover

Visibility

Present state of weather

Dewpoint

Cloud type

Height of cloud base

Cloud type

Amount of cloud

Cloud type

Barometric pressure

Barometric change in past 3 hours

Barometric tendency in past 3 hours

Pressure higher or lower than 3 hours ago

Time precipitation began or ended

Weather in past 6 hours

Amount of precipitation

balloons. The radiosonde takes readings of the temperature, barometric pressure, wind direction and relative humidity, then transmits the data to a ground receiver. These upper air observations are used in computer-based weather prediction models.

Ships and weather buoys

Ships at sea report the temperature of the sea's surface, air pressure, the ship's speed and the direction they are travelling. It is important that the ship's speed and direction are variables in the calculations because the ship's movement relative to the conditions they are reporting must be accounted for. Both moored and drifting buoys contain automated sensors that report atmospheric pressure, dry and wet bulb temperatures, wind direction and speed and sea-surface temperature.

Satellites

In April 1960, the United States launched its first satellite, the TIROS (Television and Infrared Observation Satellite), which broadcast images of clouds back to earth, allowing meteorologists to track storms. By September 1961, weather satellites had proven their usefulness by detecting the approach of Hurricane Carla, prompting the evacuation of 350,000 residents of the Texas Gulf Coast. A network of satellites, launched by various countries, comprises a global weather observation system today. Polar orbiters circle earth many times each day, observing cloud cover and reporting vertical profiles of temperature and humidity. Geosynchronous orbiters are used to gather information on wind speed and direction by tracking clouds. The orbiting speed of a geosynchronous satellite matches earth's rotation speed, so it remains over the same spot on earth's surface. One geosynchronous satellite can only see about one-quarter of earth's surface, so there are five of these satellites in orbit to build a complete picture. The European Remote-Sensing Satellite (ERS-2) uses radar to measure the roughness of the sea's sur-

Doppler radar

Doppler radar sends out radio waves that are reflected off of raindrops, snow crystals, and hailstones, then sent back to the antenna. The Doppler can detect frequency changes in these returning radio waves and determine the direction the wind is moving. Because the Doppler radar records wind velocity, it can help predict tornado outbreaks.

face, enabling forecasters to estimate sea-surface winds. Satellites collect these images using a radiometer, an instrument that records the intensity of visible radiation coming from the planet. However, detecting visible radiation is a problem at night, so satellites also use thermal infrared to obtain images of earth. By using these two methods the satellites can provide data continuously, enabling forecasters to track the movement of hurricanes, cold fronts and low-pressure cells.

Who Owns the Satellites?

Polar orbiters
● METEOR (Russia)
● NOAA (USA)

Geostationary
● GOES-W, GOES-E (USA)
● METEOSTAT (Europe)
● GMS (Japan)
● INSAT (India)

Radar

Since World War II, radar has been used to detect the location of storms, their movement and their strength. Radar sends out pulses of radio waves. These are reflected off of precipitation and bounced back to a receiver where they appear on a computer display screen. The more intense the precipitation, the more energy is returned to the receiver. The computer display screen shows the information in colour, with different colours assigned to areas of heavy and light precipitation. This radar can also detect the type of precipitation. One of the drawbacks of old-fashioned radar is that, even though it can detect the intensity and location of precipitation, it cannot indicate if tornadoes are being produced by the storm.

Doppler radar can also indicate location, movement, strength and type of precipitation, but it has the added benefit of being able to sense wind speed, wind direction and boundaries between warm and cool air. This means it can indicate the approach of a front and determine wind speeds where no rainstorms are present. Doppler radar sounds an alarm when it detects a rotating column of rising air forming because this can mean a tornado is forming.

Doppler radar works by detecting frequency changes in radio waves, which indicate wind patterns. This means that if wind is blowing the precipitation away from the Doppler antenna, the frequency of reflected radio waves is lowered. If wind is blowing the precipitation towards the Doppler antenna, the frequency of reflected radio waves is increased. When this information is displayed on a computer screen, meteorologists are provided a picture of how winds are behaving.

MAPPING THE WEATHER

A variety of measurements go into each weather map. Information is gathered from weather stations, ships at sea, weather buoys, aircraft, radar and satellites. For many years, weather maps were drawn by hand but now computers are widely used to map the weather.

Synoptic charts summarize current weather while prognostic charts predict future weather. Weather conditions for each location being mapped are plotted from data sent in from weather stations and observers. A system of symbols, which is recognized internationally, is used to plot this data.

Isobars are drawn between points of equal pressure. Closely spaced isobars are associated with low-pressure systems and indicate strong winds. When the isobars are far apart, they are associated with high-pressure systems and clear weather. High- and low-pressure systems are labelled, and areas of rainfall are often shaded. Satellite data enables the meteorologist to identify cold and warm fronts.

Dry and wet bulb thermometers

The air temperature is measured with a dry bulb thermometer that contains mercury. The mercury expands when it is heated and contracts when it is cooled. A wet bulb thermometer measures humidity. This thermometer's bulb is covered by a muslin bag, which is continuously kept wet with water supplied by a wick. The wet bulb temperature is recorded in degrees and compared to the dry bulb temperature to determine the relative humidity.

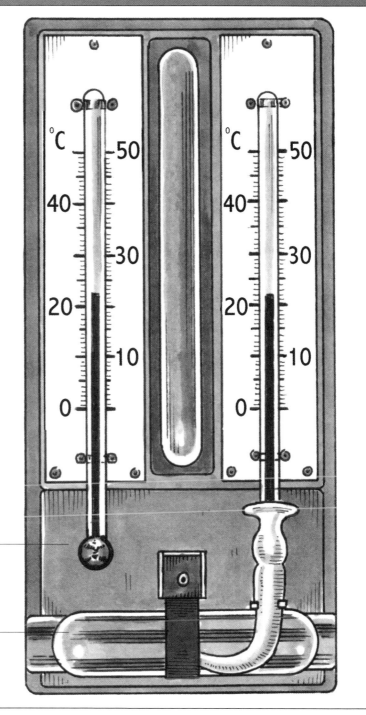

Dry bulb

Wet bulb

Computer modelling

In order to predict what the weather will do next, the meteorologist needs to know both what the atmosphere is doing currently and what physical laws govern its movements.

This is where computer modelling enters the process of forecasting. Computer models use a latitude-longitude grid with a number of levels representing different parts of the atmosphere. Meteorologists apply surface

Aneroid barometer

This type of barometer consists of a vacuum-filled metal capsule. A rise in air pressure compresses the capsule, whereas a drop in air pressure expands the capsule. This movement is sent to a series of levers, via a spring.

The levers amplify the movement to a chain that is attached to a pulley on a spindle. The pointer, which can be adjusted to give the correct reading by turning a screw, is attached to the spindle.

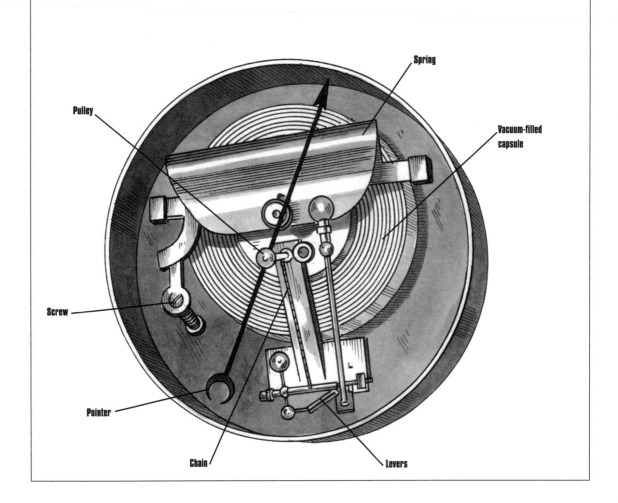

and upper air observations to this grid. There can be more than 100,000 points representing the surface conditions alone in this complex model. Surface measurements incorporate values representing temperature, wind direction and speed, humidity, soil moisture and snow cover. The model used by the European Centre for Medium-Range Weather Forecasts (ECMWF) contains 31 levels that represent layers of atmosphere that reach from earth's surface to 30.5km (19 miles) high. This is how the ECMWF's model predicts future values of temperature, wind and humidity for over four million points in earth's atmosphere. With such a large amount of data to work with, it requires a supercomputer to perform the mathematical operations necessary to forecast future conditions.

Beginning with the temperature, humidity and wind observations, the computer inserts these values into predictive equations designed to tell us how the weather will change over time. Additional data representing solar radiation intensities, variations in vegetation and temperatures at the surface of the sea, cloud behaviour and other variables are assessed. Forecasts are generated for the next 12, 24 and 48 hours and even further ahead.

Although advances in computer technology have improved forecasting capabilities, the predictions they produce are not guaranteed to be accurate. Even small changes in current conditions can affect the outcome of the forecast. This is the gamble that meteorologists face when highly accurate mathematical equations are applied to fickle nature.

Weather warnings and forecasts

Early warnings of approaching storms allow people to prepare but in order for the warnings to have value, forecasts must be disseminated rapidly. Different methods of spreading news about impending weather have been tried in history. During the late 19th century, telegraphs posted in a public place were used to communicate weather forecasts. Newspapers, too, have long published forecasts. Flags flown from where they could be seen from a distance were raised to warn of strong wind. But each of these methods had their drawbacks. In some cases many telegraph offices were closed on weekends. By the time a newspaper printed a forecast, conditions could have changed enough to render it useless. Flags, like those flown over Galveston to warn of the 1900 hurricane, could easily be overlooked or ignored.

Today the sources of information reporting what the weather might do have multiplied exponentially. Once there were only nightly television forecasts. Now there are now television channels devoted exclusively to disseminating weather information. When local television stations receive warnings about tornadoes, severe thunderstorms, hurricanes or floods, they are immediately broadcast, often interrupting normal television programming. Television viewers are accustomed to seeing satellite data and some television weather forecasters have even become celebrities. Radio stations and special emergency channels such as the NOAA weather radio also broadcast severe weather warnings. The internet, however, is emerging as one of the most popular places to retrieve information about weather conditions. Never before has so much current information on weather been so readily available. Quick access to forecasts of extreme weather saves lives and minimizes damage to property. Knowing in advance what conditions to expect allows us to prepare our homes and ourselves for the weather to come.

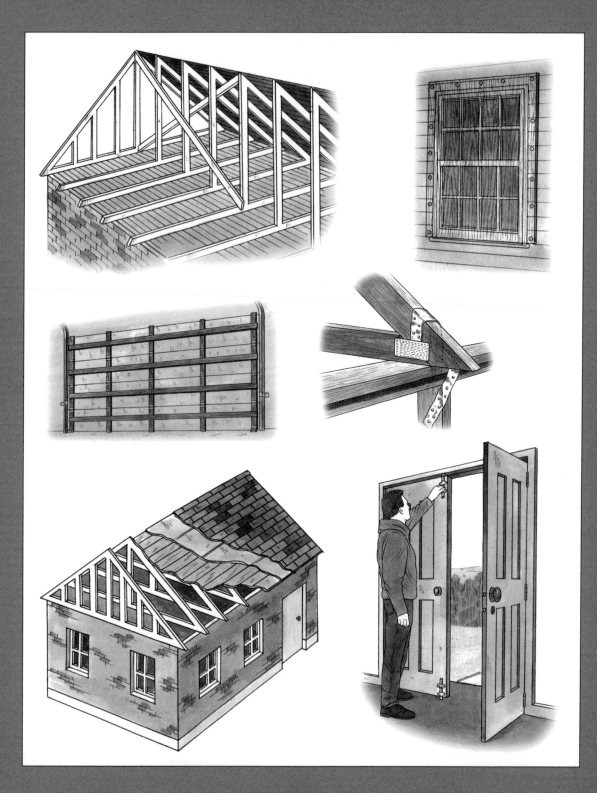

CHAPTER THREE

Protecting the Home

High winds, flooding, and extremes in hot and cold weather can damage your home. There are both permanent and temporary measures you can take to help make your home stronger, from installing effective insulation to reinforcing doors, before extreme weather strikes.

S evere weather events that affect your property cannot be prevented, but there are measures you can take to protect your home against the elements. You must first determine what risks your home faces. Are you in a flood hazard area? Is your house in a place where high winds from hurricanes or tornadoes are likely? Do you live in a mountainous area? The best way to determine potential weather threats for your area is to check with your local council's building official, city engineer, or planning and zoning administrator. You can also ask your neighbors what measures they take to protect their homes.

PROTECTING THE HOME FROM COLD
Energy efficiency

There are a number of ways to make your home more comfortable and energy efficient during the cold months. Checking your house for draughts (drafts) is a good first step. First, close all the doors and windows, as well as any fireplace dampers. Turn on any bathroom extractor fans, overhead range exhaust fans, or other fans that vent to the outside. There are specialized smoke sticks available to test for draughts (drafts), but a stick of incense will do just as well. Move the stick around your windows and doors. Unwanted currents of air will be obvious where the smoke flickers.

Be certain that all doors seal properly. Add caulk or weather stripping where appropriate, and replace any damaged weather stripping. If you own storm doors or windows, install them. Very leaky windows may need to be replaced eventually with newer, more efficient versions. A less expensive temporary alternative is to purchase a winter window insulation kit from a DIY shop (hardware store). These kits include sheets of plastic that can be cut down to fit your windows and double-faced tape to fix the plastic to the inside of your window frame. Once the plastic is taped in place, use a hair dryer to shrink the plastic until it is taut. The result is an effective way to eliminate draughts (drafts), and the plastic can easily be removed upon the arrival of spring.

Have all fireplaces inspected and cleaned. When they are not in use, shut the damper on the fireplace. Leaving the damper open on an unused fireplace creates an air current that draws warm air out of your home.

On the roof

Replace any loose or damaged shingles that could allow moisture to seep in. Any tree limbs that scrape against the roof should be trimmed back to prevent damage to the shingles. Likewise, any tree branches that could fall on your house or other structure during a storm should be cut back. Installing a screen at the top of the chimney will keep out leaves and other debris, and it will discourage birds from nesting there. Check that the flashing around your chimney or any vent pipes is in good shape and watertight. Clean rain gutters so that melting snow will have a clear path to run off. Remove ice and snow from tree limbs, the roof and any other structures once a storm has passed. Under the weight of too much snow, a roof can weaken or collapse.

Insulation

One of the most cost-efficient ways to keep a home warm is to install insulation in the attic. This is especially true in older homes where often insulation is sparse or nonexistent. Because heat rises, a significant amount of heat can be lost through the ceilings and attic.

Heating systems

Hire a professional to perform routine maintenance and inspection of your heating system. If you have propane or oil tanks, make sure they are filled before winter arrives. By cleaning dust from vents and replacing the heater's air filter each month, you significantly improve the performance and life span of your heating system. Installing a setback thermostat in your home can reduce your heating costs. These thermostats work on a timer and can be set on a schedule to automatically turn down the heat while you're asleep or away at work, then warm the house during the hours you're normally home.

Many ceiling fans have a reverse switch. When you reverse the switch on your ceiling fan, the blades blow air upwards and force the heat that has risen towards the ceiling back down into the room.

Plumbing

Any outdoor pipes that are vulnerable to freezing should be wrapped with insulation, such as heat tape. Make sure you know how to shut off water valves in your home so that any leaks that occur can be stopped immediately. Garden hose pipes should be drained, rolled up and stored indoors.

Outside the house

Cover up garden furniture or store it indoors. If you have a swimming pool, drain the filter system, cover the skimmer and cover the top of the pool. An additional coat of sealant will protect your deck from

Gabled roof

The shape of the gabled roof makes it vulnerable to the high winds produced by hurricanes or tornadoes. Gabled roofs are built with trusses that are often only held down by the plywood sheathing nailed to them. Additional bracing is necessary to strengthen these roofs against high winds.

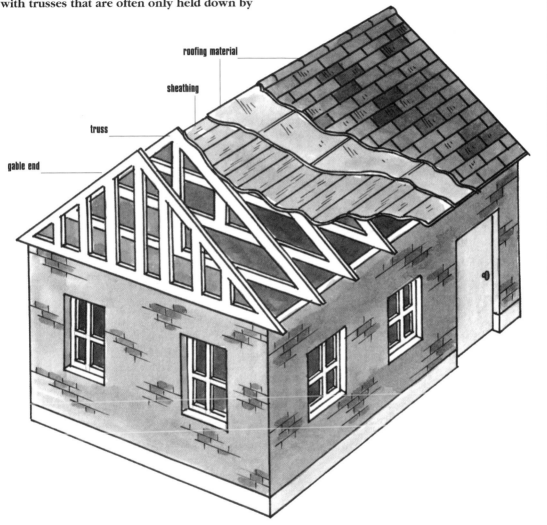

roofing material

sheathing

truss

gable end

damage.Add mulch to flowerbeds and prune shrubbery.

PROTECTING THE HOME FROM HIGH WINDS

During a tornado or hurricane high winds can severely damage your home by breaking windows and doors. In some extreme cases, the entire roof can be torn from the house. Ordinary objects in your garden may become dangerous wind-bourne projectiles. There are several are improvements you can make to your home to strengthen it against high winds, but you must embark on these projects before storm season arrives.

The roof

Most vulnerable to high winds, the roof must be properly anchored and reinforced. If the connection between the roof and walls is not strong enough, it will not be able to with-

Gabled roof after truss bracing

Truss bracing in gabled roofs consists of two-by-fours that run the length of the roof. The ends of the two-by-fours should overlap across two trusses. These braces should be installed near the ridge, in the centre span, and at the base, leaving 2.5–3m (8–10ft) between braces.

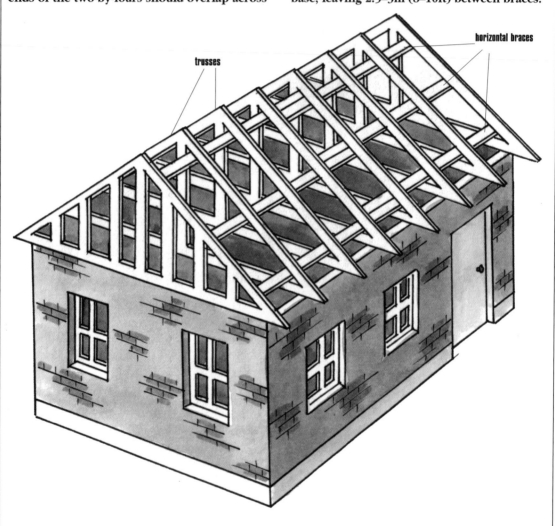

trusses

horizontal braces

stand the powerful uplift effect of strong winds and could literally be lifted off the house. Metal hurricane straps are designed to secure the roof to the exterior walls. There are also special connectors to attach a roof to a masonry wall.

Gable end roofs that are not properly braced can collapse under the pressure of high winds because the flat, A-shaped area of the gable end receives the full force of the wind. Gable end bracing is achieved by plac-

ing two-by-fours in an 'X' pattern. Position one from the bottom centre of the gable to the top centre brace of the fourth truss, and the other from the top centre of the gable to the bottom centre brace of the fourth truss.

Truss bracing, consisting of two-by-fours that run the length of the roof, should also be installed. Braces should be installed at the base, in the centre span and 46cm (18in) from the ridge, allowing 2.5–3m (8–10ft) between braces. Since a single two-by-four

Gable end bracing

Install two-by-fours in an "X" pattern for further reinforcement. The first should go from the top centre of the gable to the bottom centre brace of the fourth truss. The second should go from the bottom centre of the gable to the top center brace of the fourth truss.

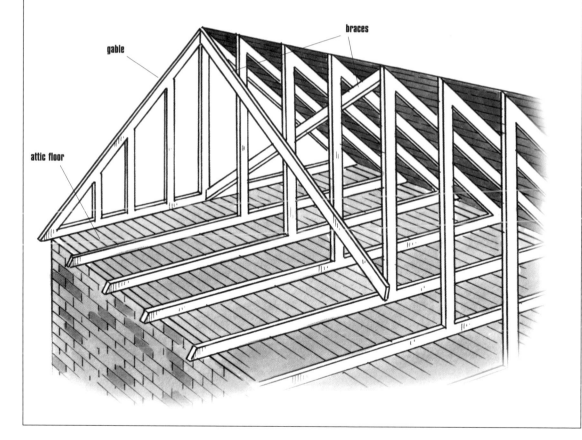

gable

braces

attic floor

Securing double entry doors

The bolts that secure most types of double entry doors are not strong enough to withstand hurricane force winds. To strengthen the doors install slide bolts at the top and bottom of the inactive door. Using longer hinge attachment screws in both doors also helps.

active door

slide bolt

inactive door

slide bolt

will not run the length of the roof, overlap the ends of the two-by-fours across two trusses.

The chimney
The taller your chimney, the more susceptible it is to high winds. Add continuous vertical reinforcing steel in the corners to provide greater wind resistance on chimneys that measure 1m (40in) or more wide or rise 1.8m (6ft) above the roofline.

Double entry doors
Double entry doors consist of an active door, which is the door that is typically used, and an inactive door, which tends to remain closed but can be opened when needed. Because these doors span twice the space of a single entry door, they are not as strong as a single door and are subsequently more vulnerable to damage caused by high winds. The bolts that secure most of these doors are not very strong. Replace the existing dead bolt with a stronger version or simply add a heavy-duty dead bolt. Add slide bolts at both the top and bottom of the inactive door.

Double-width garage doors
Double-width, or two-car, garage doors can wobble badly when buffeted by strong winds. This can cause

them to pull off their tracks or collapse. There are specially reinforced garage doors that can withstand high winds, but if you do not have this type of door, you can easily reinforce your garage door at its weakest points by installing horizontal bracing across each panel. Heavier hinges, and stronger end supports may be necessary if you brace the garage door because of the added weight of the reinforcement. Check that your garage door's track is not loose and cannot be twisted by hand. If it can be easily twisted, replace it with stronger track. Once your garage door has been reinforced, it may be out of balance. To check the balance, lower the door halfway and release it. If it moves up or down after you release it, the springs require adjusting.

Storm shutters

You can install permanent manufactured storm shutters or, if you prefer, build temporary plywood window covers to protect your windows from flying debris. All windows, including sliding glass doors, French doors and skylights, should be covered in the event of high winds. Do not forget to cover smaller windows in doors. When fitting windows for plywood shutters, add 20cm (8in) to both the

Hurricane straps

Hurricane straps made from galvanized metal are an effective and inexpensive way to help hold your roof to the walls in high winds. The straps can attach rafters to wall studs and trusses to wall studs.

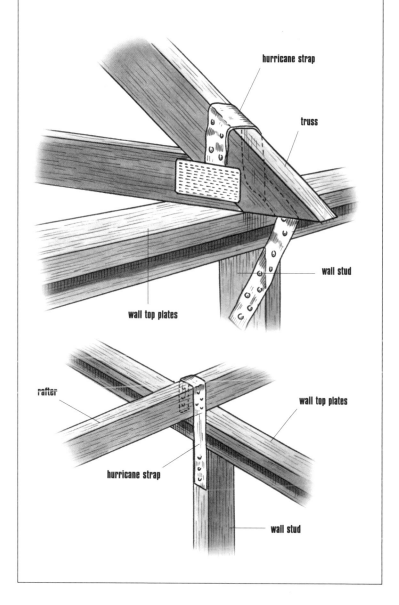

height and width measurements to allow for a 10cm (4in) overlap on each side. Drill holes for the bolts 6cm (2½in) from the outside edge of the plywood at each corner and at 30cm (12in) intervals. Drill four holes that will remain open near the centre of the plywood to relieve pressure. If you have to cover an extremely wide window, such as a picture window, you will have to use two sheets of plywood and brace it with two-by-fours. Place this bracing across the middle and bottom of the sheets of plywood.

Make sure you build the plywood shutters before storm season. Devise a numbering or lettering system so you will know which shutters fit which window. Store the shutters, along with the bolts and screws needed to mount them, in an easy-to-reach place. You will lose valuable time if you have to move heavy objects from on top of or around your stored shutters, so keep them where they can be accessed quickly.

Trees and potential wind-borne objects

High winds can topple trees and turn objects outside your home into potentially dangerous missiles. All trees should be far enough away from your house so that they cannot fall on it. Anchor storage sheds and other outbuildings either by building them on a permanent foundation or by using straps and ground anchors. Likewise, outdoor furniture, rubbish bins (garbage cans), and grills should be attached to ground anchors with cables or chain. Any fallen tree branches should be cleared away. The lids of rubbish bins (garbage cans) can be fastened on with cables or chain.

Caravans (mobile homes)

Attaching your caravan (mobile home) permanently to a foundation can decrease damages incurred from high winds. Though it does not offer as high a degree of protection as attaching your caravan (mobile home) permanently to a foundation, straps and ground anchors are preferable to no anchoring system at all.

PROTECTING YOUR HOME FROM FLOODING
Plumbing

Installing sewer back-flow valves can prevent sewage from backing up into your home through the drainpipes during a flood. Back-flow valves temporarily block pipes, which can prevent potential health hazards from occurring. Flap or

Bracing double wide garage doors

The double-width garage doors found on two-car garages wobble in high winds and pull easily off their tracks. Horizontal bracing should be installed on the inside of the garage door, along the centre of each row of door panels.

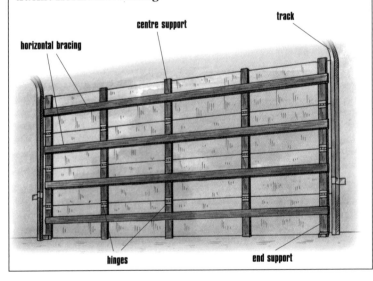

centre support

track

horizontal bracing

hinges

end support

check valves operate automatically and only allow flow out of the house, closing when flow reverses. A gate valve provides a stronger seal but, since it is manually operated, its effectiveness is dependent upon whether you had sufficient warning of the impending flood.

Fuel tanks

Floodwaters can cause unanchored fuel tanks to float, allowing them to damage the exterior of your home or other homes downstream. If the unanchored tank is in your basement, the floating tank's supply line can tear away and spill oil. An outside tank may be secured by running straps over it and attaching it to ground anchors. The best method for securing both indoor and outdoor tanks is to attach them to a large concrete slab heavy enough to resist floodwaters. The vent tube and filling tube must be above the 100-year flood level (see Chapter 4) to prevent water from entering the tank.

Electrical systems and HVAC equipment

Components of your electrical system, such as meters, outlets, circuit breaker boxes and switches can be damaged by even brief exposure to floodwaters. Floods can also cause short circuits that result in fires. Heating, ventilation and cooling (HVAC) equipment can also be damaged by floodwaters. The best way to protect these systems and equipment is to raise them above the 100-year flood level. If the furnace or hot-

Plywood storm shutters

Installing plywood storm shutters over your windows is a low-cost, effective way of protecting against flying debris during high winds. Plywood shutters should be made well before the storm season begins, marked clearly to indicate which window they fit, and stored where they can be easily reached when needed.

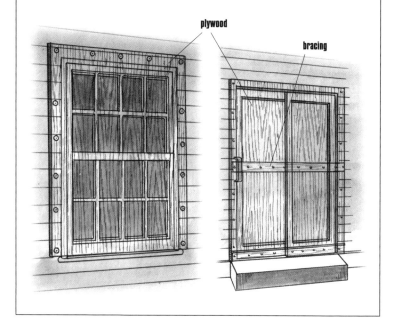

plywood

bracing

water heater cannot be moved to an upper floor or the attic, a concrete or masonry block floodwall built around them will afford a lesser degree of protection.

INSURANCE

Check that your home is insured against flooding and other damage from severe storms. Photograph or videotape your belongings and store this record, along with a list of your belongings and their value, in a secure, weatherproof location, such as a safe deposit box. Having such a record on hand will facilitate the process of filing an insurance claim in the event of lost or damaged belongings.

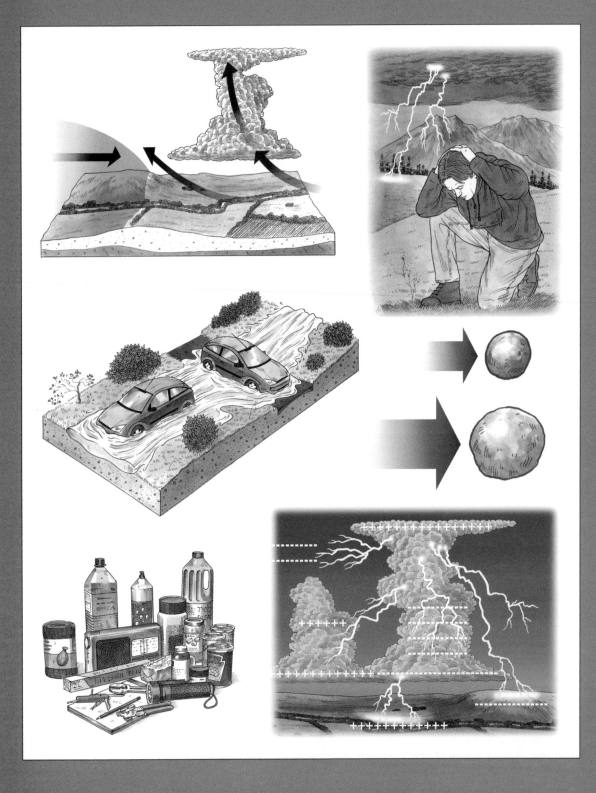

CHAPTER FOUR

Rain, Hail & Flooding

Thunderstorms can bring flash flooding, hail, and lightning. More people are killed each year by flash flooding than any other weather phenomenon. You are more likely to survive these events if you understand how suddenly these extreme weather circumstances can occur and the life-threatening consequences of them.

There are approximately 2000 storms in progress over earth at any given time. Each day about 40,000 thunderstorms rain down on our planet, but only about one per cent of them is dangerous. Lightning, hail and flooding cause severe damage to property and can even kill. Since these weather events cannot be prevented, it is important to understand how they function and recognize conditions that lead to their formation in order to protect yourself from them.

Classifying precipitation

Millions of tiny water droplets, sometimes in the form of ice crystals, go into the making of a cloud. Gravity draws them to earth in the form of liquid or frozen precipitation. What name we give to the precipitation depends upon the form it takes when it reaches the ground.

Coalescence occurs in moist cumulus-type clouds where the air temperature is above freezing. Turbulence within the cloud causes the droplets of water vapour to collide and form larger droplets that are heavy enough to fall to earth. This is how drizzle and rain occur. If the air temperature below the cloud is below freezing, the droplets can chill before reaching the ground and form freezing rain.

Types of liquid precipitation

There are two types of liquid precipitation. Drizzle consists of water droplets less than 0.5mm (0.02in) in diameter that fall close together. Rain is defined as drops larger than 0.5mm (0.02in) in diameter that are widely separated.

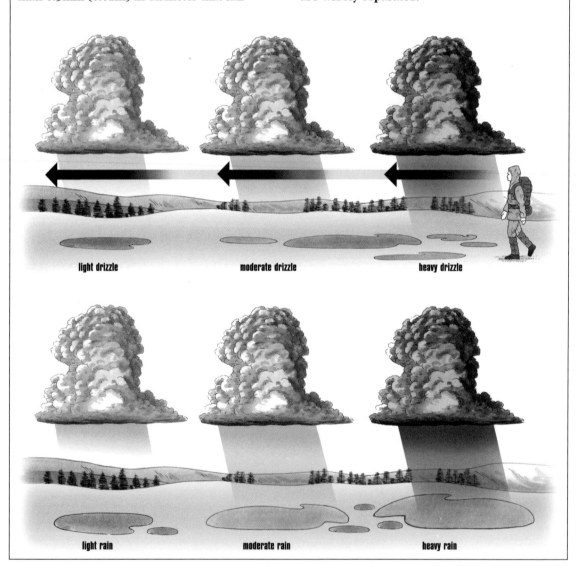

light drizzle   moderate drizzle   heavy drizzle

light rain   moderate rain   heavy rain

The Bergeron-Findeisen process, or ice-crystal process, occurs when there are both ice crystals and water droplets cooled below freezing but not yet frozen. The ice crystals attract the cold water droplets, causing them to grow larger and heavier until they fall from the cloud. As they fall through the cloud, they continue to grow through the process of coalescence. Whether or not these droplets remain frozen or melt depends on the air temperature below the cloud. If the air temperature below the cloud is below freezing, the result is dry snow or freezing rain. If the air temperature below the cloud is above freezing, the result is wet snow.

Types of liquid precipitation

Drizzle consists of tiny drops of rain with a diameter of less than 0.05cm (0.02in). These drops fall more slowly than rain and very close together.

Light drizzle: visibility of more than 0.8km ($^5/_8$ of a mile).

Moderate drizzle: visibility from 0.4–0.8km ($^5/_{16}$–$^5/_8$ mile).

Heavy drizzle: visibility of less than 0.8km ($^5/_{16}$ mile).

Precipitation and temperature

The temperature of the air below a cloud helps determine what form of precipitation falls. If the temperature below the cloud is warmer than freezing, the result is drizzle or rain. If the temperature below the cloud is freezing or colder, the result is snow or freezing rain.

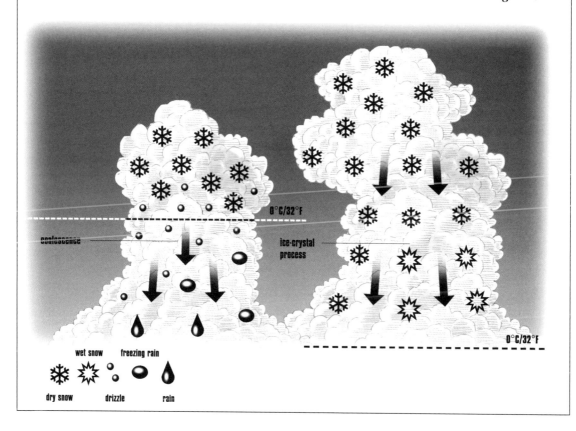

Rain consists of drops larger than 0.05cm (0.02in) in diameter or smaller drops that are widely separated.

Light rain: 0.25cm (0.1in) falls in less than an hour and the individual drops can clearly be seen.

Moderate rain: 0.28–0.76cm (0.11–0.30in) fall in an hour and drops are not easily seen.

Heavy rain: more than 0.76cm (0.30in) fall in an hour and visibility is poor because it falls in sheets.

RAIN

Thunderstorms begin as a result of unstable atmospheric conditions. The combination of warm, moist air at earth's surface and colder, denser air above it engender these storms. The first stage of a thunderstorm's formation involves the growth of a cumulus cloud as

Cold front thunderstorm

A cold front thunderstorm forms when a fast-moving wedge of cold air pushes beneath a mass of warm air. The warmer air is forced upwards where it condenses into storm-producing cumulus clouds. These thunder-storms are typically brief but violent.

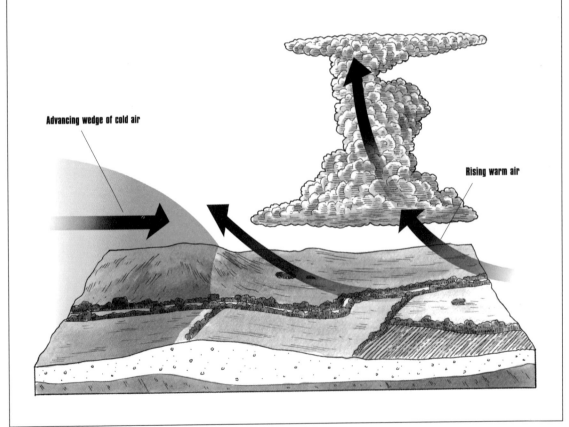

Advancing wedge of cold air

Rising warm air

the warm, moist air is lifted vertically into the cooler air. The strength of these updraughts (updrafts) prevents any rain from falling. An anvil-shaped top forms on the cloud. As the storm matures, cooler downdraughts (downdrafts) also begin to develop. The moisture in these cooler, denser downdraughts (downdrafts) colliding with the moisture in the updraughts (updrafts) causes rain to fall. The final stage involves the cooler downdraughts (downdrafts) cutting off the supply of warm updraughts (updrafts), causing the cloud to separate. Cirrus and altocumulus clouds may form above the dissipating cumulus cloud.

Cold-front rain

Cold fronts tend to produce some of the heaviest rainfall. The colder, heavier air displaces warm air by shoving underneath it and rapidly forcing the warm air upwards. Unless the air is dry, cumulonimbus clouds form and grow into thunderstorms.

Warm-front rain

Warm air moves into an area with cold air, rises above the cold air, then cools. Condensation occurs and clouds form. Cirris clouds are the first to form at the head of the front, followed by thick, low-level nimbostratus clouds that produce rain.

Sea-coast rain

The sea and the land cool off and heat up at different rates. The land absorbs more heat during the daytime and releases

Warm front thunderstorm

As warm air advances over a retreating wedge of cold air, a warm front thunderstorm forms. Because warm fronts travel more slowly than cold fronts, the uplift of warm air is more gradual and accompanied by less turbulence. Warm front thunderstorms are less severe than cold front thunderstorms.

Warm air

Retreating wedge of cold air

Sea coast thunderstorm

Oceans are much slower to warm and cool than landmasses. The land absorbs more heat during the day than the adjacent water, and at night the land radiates more heat than the water. As warm air over land rises, moist air from the ocean moves beneath it. This moist air heats up, ascends, and forms thunderclouds.

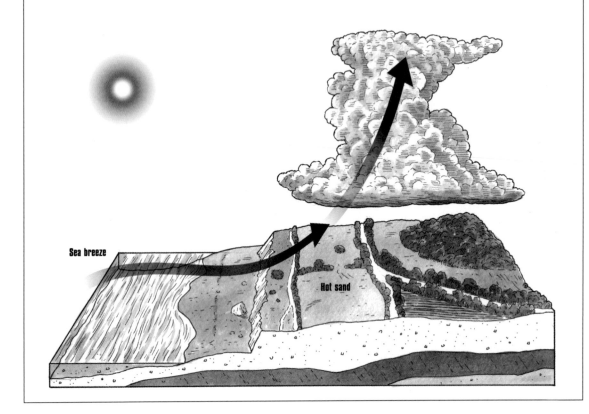

Sea breeze

Hot sand

more heat at night than the sea does. The sea cools and warms up more slowly, giving it a more stable temperature. Warm air rises over the warm land during the day, and moist, cooler air from the sea blows in to replace it. Once it is over the warmer land, the cool air heats up, rises and forms thunderclouds.

Mountain rain
Moist air carried by a prevailing wind is forced upwards when it encounters a mountain. As the air rises the water vapour condenses, clouds form and rain occurs.

Terms associated with precipitation
Squall line: a line of gusty thunderstorms that precede a cold front pushing into warm, moist air and may appear as a wave of rolling black clouds.

Cloudburst: sudden, heavy downpour of rain that falls in a sheet instead of distinguishable drops

Thunder squall: a strong, cool wind emitted from the lower front part of an approaching thundercloud.

Thunderhead: the anvil-shaped top of a mature cumulonimbus cloud.

Virga: this is a dark fringe of evaporating precipitation that hangs from the cloud base. It is caused by a layer of dry air beneath the cloud.

Microbursts

A microburst is a narrow column of cold air that blasts down out of a cloud, sometimes at speeds of 240km (150 miles) per hour or greater. Microbursts present an extreme hazard to aviators, and have caused many accidents. As elusive as they are dangerous, they cover an area of less than 3km (2 miles) and normally last for less than ten minutes. Their most severe winds last less than four minutes.

Mountain thunderstorm

Mountains form natural barriers to winds. As moist air is forced upwards by a mountain, it condenses and forms thunderclouds. This upwards movement is helped along by updrafts rising from the sun-warmed slopes. These mountain thunderstorms are also called orographic storms.

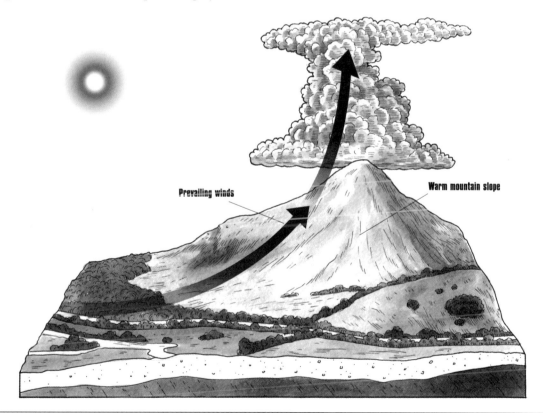

Prevailing winds

Warm mountain slope

Cumulonimbus cloud

Cumulonimbus clouds produce heavy rain, thunder, lightning, and sometimes hail. These clouds are taller than they are wide, and they have a flat base and sharp outline. Cumulonimbus clouds form as moist air rises in updrafts, cools, and condenses. Its anvil-shaped head is a sure sign of a thunderstorm. When the cool air reaches the top of the cloud, gravity and precipitation cause it to descend in downdrafts.

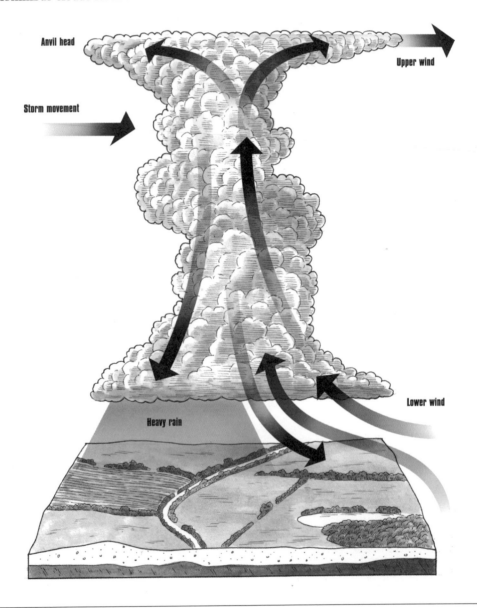

Anvil head

Upper wind

Storm movement

Lower wind

Heavy rain

Dry microbursts

Dry microbursts are caused when the air below a shower or thunderstorm is very dry and the rain evaporates into the dry air. This has a cooling effect on the air. The now heavier cooled air plunges to the ground. When it strikes the ground, the air spreads out in all directions, causing wind shear. Sometimes the only visual evidence that a dry microburst is occurring is the sight of clouds of dust kicked up by the wind.

Wet microbursts

Wet microbursts occur when dry air enters a thunderstorm. This causes the rain to evapo-rate, which cools the dry air rapidly. The newly cooled heavier air plunges to the ground. These wet microbursts can often be hidden by rainfall.

LIGHTNING

Lightning is one of the deadliest natural phe-nomena, second only to flooding in terms of how many lives are lost to it each year. A bolt of lightning is 28,000°C (50,000°F), almost five times hotter than the sun's 6090°C (11,000°F) surface. Lightning occurs when electricity courses between two areas of oppositely charged particles. It manifests as cloud-to-air lightning, in-cloud lightning,

Thunderstorm probability

It is possible to predict the probability of a thunderstorm by using only a barometer and wet bulb thermometer. A high wet bulb temperature combined with a drop in baro-metric pressure increases the probability of a thunderstorm.

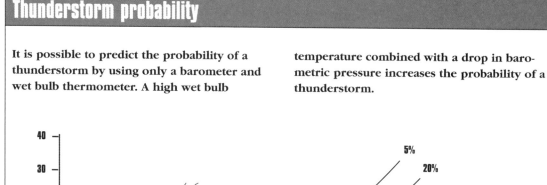
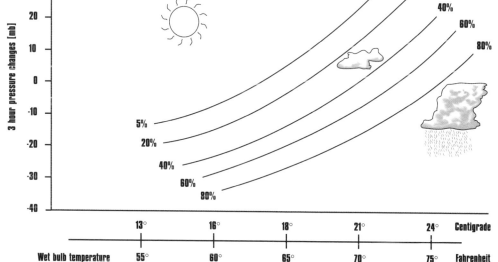

Life cycle of a storm

The developing stage of a thunderstorm involves several stages. To begin with warm, humid air rises as updrafts. This is leads to condensation occurring and clouds forming In its mature stage, the top of the cloud spreads out and cool air descends as downdrafts, accompanied by precipitation. The cooler downdrafts eventually block the supply of warm, ascending air, and the storm dissipates.

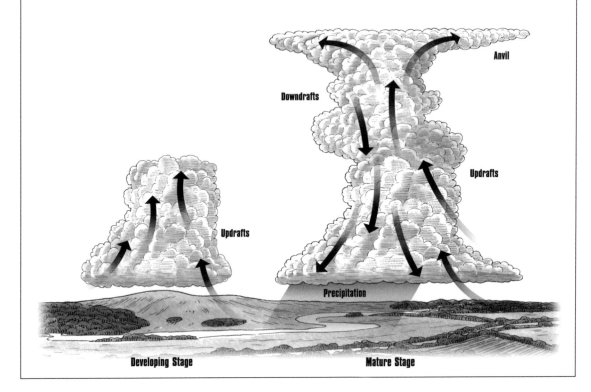

Anvil

Downdrafts

Updrafts

Updrafts

Precipitation

Developing Stage

Mature Stage

cloud-to-cloud lightning, and cloud-to-ground lightning.

Earth's surface normally carries a negative charge, but a passing thunderstorm with a negative charge in its base will cause a positive charge to build up on the ground below. This new positive charge will follow the cloud as it moves. The air between the positively charged ground and the negatively charged bottom of the cloud will insulate the opposing charges from one another until these charges become so strong they can no longer be kept apart. A stepped leader of negatively charged electrons is sent down from the cloud. When it nears the ground, it attracts a positively charged streamer up through a high point, such as a tree or tall building. As the stepped leader and the streamer meet, a powerful electrical current of up to 100 million volts flows as a return stroke, travelling upwards towards the cloud at about 96,500km (60,000 miles) per second. With all that heat the air pressure around the lightning stroke rises, causing the air to rapidly expand in a shock wave that is heard as thunder.

Types of lightning

There are several types of lightning, but all lightning occurs between opposing electrical charges. Lightning can occur from cloud to ground, from cloud to air, between two clouds, or within one cloud. Only about one in four lightning bolts strikes the ground. A bolt that travels all the way from the positively charged top of the cloud to a negatively charged area that is not directly beneath the cloud is called a positive flash.

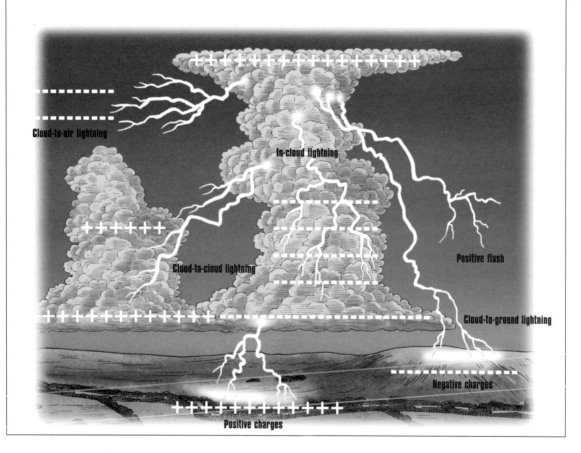

Cloud-to-air lightning

In-cloud lightning

Cloud-to-cloud lightning

Positive flash

Cloud-to-ground lightning

Negative charges

Positive charges

Lightning strikes that occur closer to you have thunder that makes a cracking noise. The thunder from strikes farther away sounds like a boom or rumble because the sound has been reflected off of many objects, such as hills and buildings, before reaching your ears. It takes sound three seconds to travel one kilometre (five seconds to travel one mile). To estimate the distance between you and a lightning strike, count the seconds that elapse between seeing the lightning and hearing the thunderclap. Divide the number of seconds by three to estimate the lightning's distance in kilometres (or by five to determine the distance in miles). The sound from a lightning strike will not travel more than about 24 kilometres (15 miles).

Types of lightning

Streak: this form of lightning has a zigzag shape. Streak lightning occurs as lines or streaks between two clouds or between ground and cloud.

Forked: streak lightning that forms two or more branches at the same time.

Ribbon: streak lightning that has been blown sideways by high wind, forming separate, parallel streaks that are seen as a series of bands or ribbons.

Heat: flickers above the horizon where no thunderclouds are present, possibly the reflection of lightning occurring below the horizon.

Sheet: hidden lightning that travels from cloud to cloud, illuminating an expanse of cloud like a sheet of light. This is one of the most common forms of lightning.

Bead: also called pearl necklace or chain lightning, the brightness along its path varies, giving the appearance of a string of beads. This type of lightning is very rare and almost impossible to photograph.

St Elmo's Fire: a mass of sparks that forms when opposite charges are too weak to generate a lightning bolt, often seen near the top of ships' masts or noses of aircraft.

Lightning myths

It is only a myth that lightning will never

Evolution of a lightning stroke

Negatively charged electrons zigzag downwards in a forked pattern known as a stepped leader. Near the ground, the stepped leader draws a positively charged streamer upwards. A powerful electrical current begins to flow as the leader and streamer meet. The return stroke, a positive charge traveling upwards at one-third the speed of light, creates the light we see as the flash.

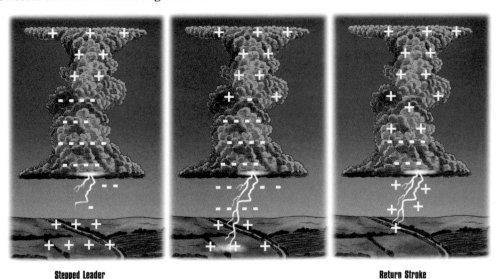

Stepped Leader   Return Stroke

strike twice in the same place. Lightning can strike several times in the same place during the course of one discharge. Many people also believe that if it is not raining, lightning poses no danger. The fact is, lightning can occur as far as 16 kilometres (10 miles) away from rainfall. Rubber-soled shoes and rubber tires on cars have long been thought to protect people from lightning but they provide no protection whatsoever. However, the steel frame of a hard-topped vehicle provides increased protection as long as you are not touching metal inside the car. It is still possible to be injured by lightning while inside a car, but you are much safer inside the car than outside.

Survivor's story

Steve Ely survived being struck by lightning on a Florida golf course in August 1977. He was carrying a metal-tipped umbrella and a bag of metal golf clubs. His golf shoes had metal spikes. All of these accessories made him a veritable lightning rod.

'I remember a blinding flash of light and just this indescribable feeling of having something go through my body and knock me to the ground. I don't know if it knocked me out or not, but it couldn't have been for that long. I remember coming to just lying on the ground, *disoriented, with no feeling in my body. For a brief moment, I thought to myself that I might be dead.*

I quickly realized what had happened,

Squatting position when lightning threatens

If caught out in the open during a lightning storm with no shelter, squat low to the ground as quickly as possible. Do not lie flat on the ground.

The aim is to get as low as possible while minimizing the area of exposed body surface. Lying flat makes you a larger target.

but still had no feeling and thought that I must be completely paralyzed. The guy in the pro shop had seen it happen and had already called an ambulance. My brother had been knocked down by the force of the lightning, even though he was 200 yards (183m) behind me. When he came up on me, I was pretty hysterical, and he took off running for the pro shop to get help.

My dad had just arrived at the course with some friends of his, with plans to play also (after the weather cleared). When they heard the news, they took off in the car for where I was. There was a small road that ran just off the first fairway, and some guys driving by in a truck had come out to get me and were carrying me back to their truck when my father arrived.

He got me and put me in the back of the car and one of his buddies started driving us to the hospital. Around this time, I started getting the feeling back in my legs, with this unbelievable pain that was from the tremendous muscle contractions caused by the lightning. I still thought I might be paralyzed above the waist but soon that feeling started coming back.

Then I began to notice this pain in my right palm and saw why: the crease running through my palm near my thumb was completely opened up. However, there was no blood because, I found out later, it was cauterized by the lightning. An ambulance met us on the way to the hospital and now I got loaded into that. I remember them just asking me some basic questions, I guess to see if I was in shock.

When we got to the hospital, my heart rate was beating about 200 beats a minute. They soon go that under control and began to work on the other injuries. They used about a dozen stitches on my right palm to close it up (you can still see the scar from that injury), and then began to notice the burns that went all the way down my body. There were just some spotty burns until you got to my feet, where there were pretty serious third-degree burns on the tops of my feet. You could see where the lightning went out between my toes. My shirt and shorts had holes in them, and my socks and shoes were really torn up. The umbrella was completely torn up. They kept me in the hospital for a few days to observe my heart and to care for the burns on my feet, and I was on crutches for a couple more weeks.'

There are health effects associated with surviving a lightning strike. They include:
- Chronic Fatigue
- Long-term memory loss
- Short-term memory loss
- Irritability
- Severe headaches
- Seizures
- Loss of motor skills
- Depression
- Cognitive thinking impairment
- Radical personality changes
- Ticks or uncontrollable muscular movement
- Stiffness in joints
- Anxiety or panic attacks
- Sleep disturbances
- Diminished sex drive

SURVIVING LIGHTNING
Before a storm
- Listen to news and weather forecasts.
- Be aware of any flood warnings
- Make sure animals have aplace to shelter.
- Have an emergency supply kit on hand.

Emergency Supplies Kit
- Portable, battery-powered radio
- Torch (Flashlight)
- Manual can opener
- Emergency food and water
- First aid kit and manual
- Cash and credit cards
- Sturdy shoes

Safe refuges from lightning

During a thunderstorm the safest place to be is in a low-rise building. Keep the windows closed and unplug any electrical equipment. If you can't take refuge in a building, a car is a safe alternative. If a car (or airplane for that matter) is hit by lightning you will not be harmed. However, avoid touching any metal parts of the interior, such as the radio.

Unsafe refuges from lightning

Standing in an open field, on a golf course or beach, or under a tree are all the wrong places to be when lightning strikes. Lightning is attracted to tall targets. If you feel your hair standing on end, lightning is about to strike near you.

Thunderstorm watches and warnings

When authorities issue a severe thunderstorm watch it means that the conditions are favourable for severe thunderstorms and lightning over a broad area. When a severe thunderstorm warning is issued, it means that a severe thunderstorm has been spotted locally. It is important to take thunderstorm warnings seriously – in the U.S. there are more deaths caused by lightning each year than by any other natural disaster, Worldwide there are approximately 1000 deaths caused by lightning annually.

During a storm

- Do not use the phone.
- Unplug appliances, including the television.
- Do not bathe, shower or run water. Electricity can be conducted through metal pipes.
- Turn off air-conditioning units to protect them from power surges.
- Take cover in a car or building and close the windows.
- If you are in the woods, stand under the shortest trees.
- If you are in a boat or swimming, get to land immediately and seek shelter.
- Listen to a battery-powered radio for news updates.
- Stay away from tall trees, metal objects or poles.
- Squat low to the ground, tuck your head between your knees and put your hands on your knees. If you feel a tingling sensation in your skin or sense that your hair is standing on end, it is an indication that lightning is about to strike near you.
- Remain calm.

After a storm

- Administer first aid to anyone who needs it. Remember that lightning strike victims do not retain an electrical charge; it is safe to touch them. Give the victim CPR if his or her heart has stopped.
- Report any damaged power lines to the utility company.
- Contact your insurance agent to report any lightning damage to your property so you can file a claim.
- If you are away from your home, do not attempt to return there until confirmed reports on road damage and emergency routes have been issued.

HAIL

Hail is the largest and heaviest type of precipitation. It destroys crops, damages cars and houses and, in extreme cases, has been known to be fatal to animals and humans. A hailstorm in Bangladesh in 1986 produced hailstones weighing more than one kilogram (two pounds) and killed 92 people. Larger hailstones can literally pummel you to death or bury you under a drift of hailstones where you can die of cold and exposure. Hail is difficult to forecast, so hailstorms almost invariably arrive unexpectedly.

Hail consists of concentric-layered balls of ice. It forms when a small particle of ice circulated through a cumulonimbus cloud on updraughts (updrafts) and downdraughts (downdrafts) collides with other ice particles and grows larger and heavier. The faster the updraught (updraft), the larger the potential hailstones. Hail is released from the cloud when it grows too heavy for the updraughts (updrafts) to support it. You can actually cut a hailstone in half and examine its layers to determine how many circuits of the cloud the hail made during its formation as each layer represents one trip through the cloud. Hailstones comprised of as many as 25 ice layers have been recorded.

Types of hail

Graupel: soft, round, opaque hail about the size of peas with the consistency of tiny snowballs.

Small: has a graupel centre surrounded by a thin layer of ice and is relatively transparent.

True: larger than graupel and small hail, it has layers of ice and snow surrounding its nucleus.

Survivor's story

Gina Montgomery Brewer encountered a violent hailstorm in Jal, New Mexico in the early 1960s.

'The hail began as innocent little pea-sized, mush balls… The ground began to quickly get wet and the road was covered with white mush. Suddenly we heard a thud! The hail had grown into golf-ball size and was coming down hard and fast! My dad unexpectedly stopped the car and dashed out to scoop up a small boy off the sidewalk as he was frantically running trying to dodge the hailstones that had begun to get larger and larger.

The last half block was terrifying! My dad slid into our carport and we all dashed wide-eyed into the house where my mother, grandmother and sisters stood gazing out the windows. Surely the worst was over! My grandmother stood peering out the kitchen window, wringing a corner of her apron and staring at her brand new 1962 Chevy Nova that had just made its maiden voyage to Jal. She watched as the hailstones grew from golf-ball, to baseball, to grapefruit size. She winced as the huge globs of ice mutilated her shiny new car. She cried as she realized that there was nothing anyone could do except watch it happen. My poor frustrated dad just stood watching it all, rolling his stub of a cigar from one side of his mouth to the other as if he had mistakenly put in the lit end and was trying to find a comfortable spot for it. My mother was, as always, the calm force amidst the storm and chaos - assuring all of us it would pass very soon.

Suddenly, with a great menacing gust the wind whipped our small evaporative cooler from the window in the living room. In a fit of fear… my cousin and I were leaping over the huge grapefruit hailstones that came flying through the window. (Must have been a comical sight - we were like bowling pins that the storm was trying to knock over.) Every window on the south side of our house was gone and still the rain and hail came down. The sound of it was like a great herd of buffalo trampling the roof, and we were quite sure there would be nothing left of our little flat-topped house.

Then, as suddenly as it began, the rain and hail stopped. Almost simultaneously everyone in the neighbourhood exited their homes to inspect the damage. There were flooded yards, broken trees, shattered glass, crumpled fences, destroyed vehicles and an echo among neighbours as they yelled to each other, "Is everyone all right at your place?"'

SURVIVING HAIL

Since hail occurs so suddenly and lasts for such a short time, there is not much you can do to prepare yourself for it. The only way to protect yourself from hail is to take shelter immediately at the first signs of hail and remain there until the storm passes. Move your car into a garage or under a carport to protect its windows and finish.

FLOODING

Floods can be divided into two categories: flash flooding and broad-scale flooding. The soil cannot effectively absorb rain that falls at a rate of more than 2.5cm (1in) an hour. The rain runs off instead, causing erosion, damaging buildings, destroying crops and drowning both people and animals. A sudden flood can crash through canyons or pour through desert gullies, washing away cars, roads, bridges and homes that stand in its path. Mudslides can be set in motion. Cities are susceptible because they are composed of large areas of concrete and asphalt, which do not absorb rain. The hard, dry soil of the desert does not easily absorb water, a fact that contributes to flash flooding. In North American deserts where unexpected torrents can come crashing down dry creek beds, statistically, more people drown than die from thirst. Flash flooding kills more people yearly than any other natural disaster. Because these floods occur so abruptly,

Wind speed and the size of hailstones

How fast the winds in a thunderstorm's updrafts are traveling helps determine how large hailstones will be. These are examples of the approximate upward wind speeds required to produce various sizes of hailstone.

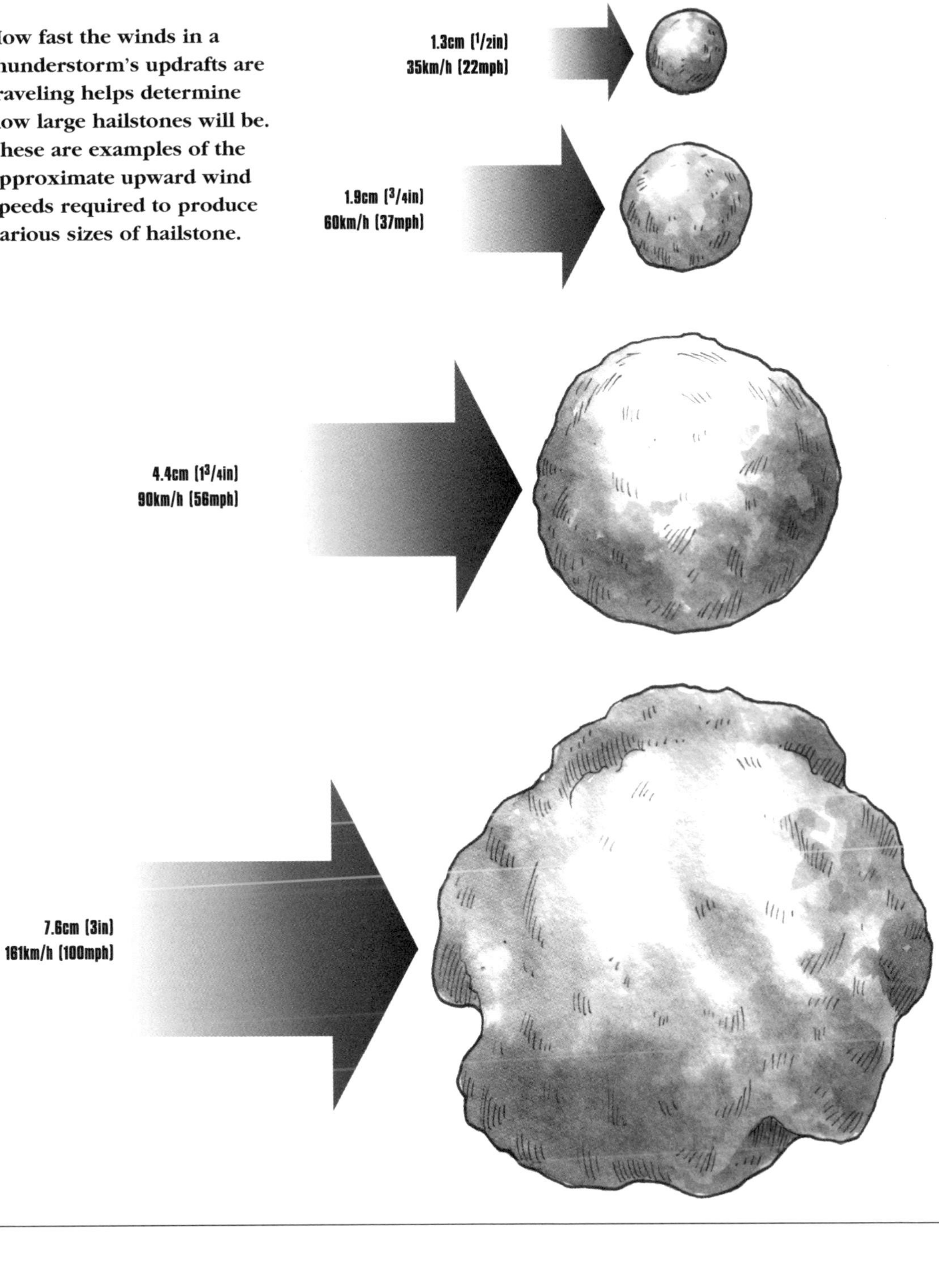

1.3cm (¹/₂in)
35km/h (22mph)

1.9cm (³/₄in)
60km/h (37mph)

4.4cm (1³/₄in)
90km/h (56mph)

7.6cm (3in)
161km/h (100mph)

people in the vicinity normally have very little warning that the flood is approaching.

While flash floods are devastating, their waters recede quickly and their effects are normally felt over a relatively small area. Broad-scale flooding is produced by a frontal system that unleashes rains over an extended area for a greater length of time. Rivers and streams, unable to carry the sudden surplus of water, overflow their banks and leave cities and farms standing in deep water. Every spring when the melting winter snow is combined with rainfall, flooding occurs. A hurricane can also cause significant broad-scale flooding because of its accompanying storm surge that forces large amounts of water inland over soil that is already saturated.

The monsoon season of southern Asia heralds an abrupt change from dry weather to torrential rains and flooding. The monsoons bring massive amounts of rain and cause flooding in an area where flooding from cyclones is already a threat.

100-Year Floods

Engineers use the term '100-year flood' to describe how high flood levels should reach, on average, once a century. It is possible, and not entirely unusual, to have a 100-year flood more than once a century. It is also not unusual for an area to go for 200 years without experiencing a 100-year flood. The number is a statistical average. One way to think about the 100-year flood level is that there is a one per cent chance of it occurring each year.

A car: the wrong place to be

Many victims of floods die in their vehicles while trying to outrun the rising water. Others die trying to escape vehicles that suddenly become inundated with water. Standing water on a road can hide large holes where segments of pavement have been washed away. Floodwater moving at

only 6.5km (4 miles) per hour exerts a force of around 300kg per sq m (66lbs per sq ft) on any objects in its path. If the same water is moving at 13km (8 miles) per hour, the force it exerts rises dramatically to 1200kg per sq m (264lbs per sq ft). Add the force of the moving water to the fact that it takes less than 60cm (2ft) of water to float a car, and you will understand how a car can be washed off the road by what looks like a navigable amount of water.

Survivor's story

Larry Conn survived the 1972 Buffalo Creek Flood in West Virginia. The flood was a result of a dam break, and it devastated the mining community downstream.

The radio announcer was always talking, this morning though, Bill Beckerer, the owner of the radio station and all of them were saying that the dam was broken and homes were coming down stream and the Buffalo residents needed to evacuate or get to higher ground. We heard this so many times before; the dam was breaking, it didn't make us run for the hills scared because we had heard them cry wolf so much, we thought it was just another scare tactic.

The reports kept coming, people running on top of roof tops, couldn't get off, people floating downstream on mattresses, tops of roads, homes washing away, "evacuate the area immediately", he kept saying.

We still never felt like there was anything to be afraid of, so I opened the door and looked out. Everybody was evacuating. I told Dad, he was still a little tipsy, I said, "Dad, Mom, everyone is leaving."

Dad said to take the kids and go to higher grounds but I still didn't know, so higher ground was stepping out of the house and walking up the hill, no shelter or anything. My dad said to get us to higher ground. So, me and my mama and eight more children headed up towards the dam. We went to a place called Accoville. We went up on Accoville Flat but when we got to go up to the road water was over the road, so we went up on a flat at Accoville, parked the car and got out and watched.

From Accoville Flat you can look down and see the whole community and you could suddenly see a wall, a big wave of water come. It was black and you could see it as it came, the houses exploded like they were dynamited. They just exploded and house trailers were moving like boats in a swimming pool. This great wall of water was bringing everything down with it.

The power lines began to shake where there were the houses in front of us; washing bridges away, watching all of this devastation. Washing away my friends' houses, watching everybody left.

I had some friends with me, Bob Jude and Kenny McCoy. We begin to walk up the road. The water receded as quickly as it came, boom! boom! Once the dam water had passed, it receded and went right down. There was no more flood, like pouring a bucket of water out.

We begin to walk up the road, there

Car washed away by less than two feet of water

A car begins to float when the water around it is less than 0.6m (2ft) deep. Moving water's momentum is transferred to the car. For each foot (0.3m) the water rises, 225kg (500lbs) of lateral force are applied to the car.

Once the car becomes buoyant, the force of the water can wash it away into deeper water.

The force of water

Moving water is extremely dangerous. An adult can be knocked down by 15.2cm (6in) of moving water, and even small waves can cause extensive damage to buildings and property. On the night of 31 January 1953, a combination of strong winds and low pressure caused waves of up to 3.3m (11ft) in the North Sea to batter the coast. In the Netherlands 50 dykes burst, 1800 people drowned and 9 per cent of agricultural land was flooded. In England 307 people drowned and over 90,000 hectares (220,000 acres) of land was flooded.

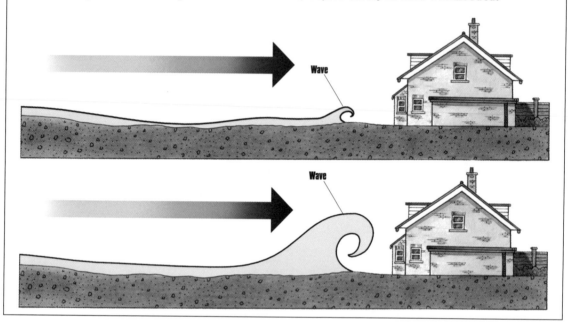

were bodies everywhere. They were not laying out like a battlefield, but one stuck here, one in a bridge, one in the schoolyard. They found my neighbour, an elderly, sick man, who was spending the night with his daughter, he washed out of the house. We found him in the schoolyard. We found him, Mr Breabole, dead.'

The devastation caused by the flood resembled a scene from a horror story. As Larry surveyed his neighbourhood the extent of the destruction became increasingly evident.

'As I traveled out the alley towards my home, my neighbour's garage and parts of other homes blocked us from entering our driveway. When we finally crawled our way into the yard our house was flooded. Our home was bad. We could not stay in our house, so we made our way to grandmother's home. I stayed in the shelter at school, to make room for other members of my family at my grandmother's home.

I went then to Fred Osborne's home in Kistler on Buffalo Creek to stay. My friend Roy Bruce Browning was there he lost everything. His wife Donna and his child Brucie were both drown in the flood. Those nights were like a bad dream. We would make trips to the temporary morgue to see if his wife and son had been found. One day she was found and not long after that *his son was found. This was tragic. I remember lots of funerals, members of all those families buried. It was bad.'*

SURVIVING FLOODS
Before flooding occurs

- Take steps to flood-proof your home (as discussed earlier.
- Check with local emergency authorities to ascertain if your home is in the flood plain.
- Purchase flood insurance. Homeowner's insurance does not cover flood damage.
- Agree on a place outside of the flood plain where your family can go in case evacuation is necessary. This can be the home of a friend or relative, a shelter or a motel located on higher ground.
- Ask a friend or relative who lives outside of the flood area to agree to be a family contact. It is often easier to make a long-distance call after a flood. Be sure that everyone in the family knows the contact's name, address and phone number. This will help family members reunite in case they are separated during the flood.
- Make sure that everyone in the family knows how to respond to a flood warning.
- Teach everyone in the family how and when to turn off the gas, electricity and water.
- If they are not tied down securely, store rubbish bins (garbage cans), lawn furniture and grills indoors.
- Move valuable possessions, such as photographs, legal papers and jewellery upstairs.
- Plot several evacuation routes on a map. One is not enough because the floodwaters may have rendered it impassable. Alternatives are a must.
- Store emergency supplies where they can be retrieved easily.
- Use stoppers to plug the drain in the shower and bathtub. This prevents flood-waters from coming into your home through the plumbing.
- Fill your bathtub and any available containers with clean water. Sterilize sinks and bathtubs using bleach. Rinse them out thoroughly before filling them with water for drinking. Water service may be interrupted.
- Make certain you have sandbags in case you have to construct a dyke (dike) to protect your home.
- Keep a current map in the car and one in your emergency supply kit.
- Fill the tank of your car with fuel.
- Pay attention to flood warnings. Monitor television or radio newscasts.
- If you evacuate, take pets with you.

EMERGENCY SUPPLIES
Water

It helps to keep 13.5 litres (3 gallons) of water on hand for each member of your household. Store the water in clean plastic containers. Replace it with fresh water every six months. If you are caught without a supply of clean drinking water, you can melt ice cubes or use the water in your hot water tank. As a last resort, use the water in your toilet tank. Do not use the water in the toilet bowl.

If none of those emergency water sources are available, you can purify contaminated water by boiling it for five minutes. Or you can add sixteen drops of household bleach per 4.5 litres (gallon) of water, stir, and let it stand for 30 minutes.

Food

Because utility service may be interrupted, store at least a three-day supply of non-perishable food. Choose foods that need no cooking, refrigeration or preparation. Rotate food items once a year.

- Tinned juices, milk and soup
- High energy foods such as peanut butter,

muesli (granola) bars, dried fruit and nuts, biscuits
- Ready-to-eat tinned meats, fruits and vegetables
- Vitamins
- Special foods infants or the elderly might require
- Biscuits (cookies), boiled sweets (hard candy), sweetened cereal, tea bags, instant coffee
- Manual can opener
- Paper plates, plastic cups and cutlery, or camping mess kits
- Washing up liquid (liquid detergent)
- Aluminium foil and paper kitchen towels
- Non-perishable pet food

First Aid Kit
- Various sizes of adhesive bandages
- Various sizes of sterile gauze pads
- Adhesive tape
- Triangular bandages
- Sterile rolled bandages
- Cotton wool and swabs
- Scissors
- Tweezers
- Sewing needle
- Antiseptic
- Iodine
- Thermometer
- Soap
- Assorted sizes of safety pins
- Moist wipes
- Rubber (latex) gloves
- Sun block
- Insect repellent
- Aspirin or other pain reliever
- Prescription medications
- Anti-diarrhoea medicine
- Laxative
- Antacid

Clothes and personal items
- A change of clothing, sturdy shoes, rain gear
- Blankets or sleeping bags

- Extra set of car keys
- Toilet paper
- Toiletry and personal hygiene items
- Extra pair of glasses or contact lenses and supplies
- Credit cards and cash
- Books
- Toys for children

Pets
- If you evacuate your home, do not leave pets behind. Even if they do survive the storm, they may be frightened enough to run away.
- Be sure that identification tags have current information and are securely attached to your pet's collar.
- Have a secure pet carrier, lead (leash) or harness for your pet so if he panics, he can't run away.
- Keep a current photo of your pet in case he gets lost.
- Never ever leave your pet chained outside during a storm.
- Pack a pet survival kit in advance.
- Many emergency shelters do not allow pets. Find out well in advance which hotels allow pets.
- If there is absolutely no alternative but leaving your pet at home when you evacuate, confine your pet to a safe area indoors. Select an easily cleaned area, such as a utility room or bathroom. Do not choose a room with windows. The room should have counters to provide higher ground for the pet in case water rises in the room. Establish two separate rooms if you have dogs and cats. Put a note on the front door indicating what pets are in the house and where they are located. Write your contact number and the number of the vet who looks after your pet on the note.

Pet survival kit
- Non-perishable pet food

Survival kit

A survival kit should include a torch (flashlight), battery-powered radio, bottled water, tinned food, aluminum foil, vitamins, dishwashing liquid, bleach, a manual can opener, a utility knife, wrench, paper and pencil, and rubbish (garbage) bags.

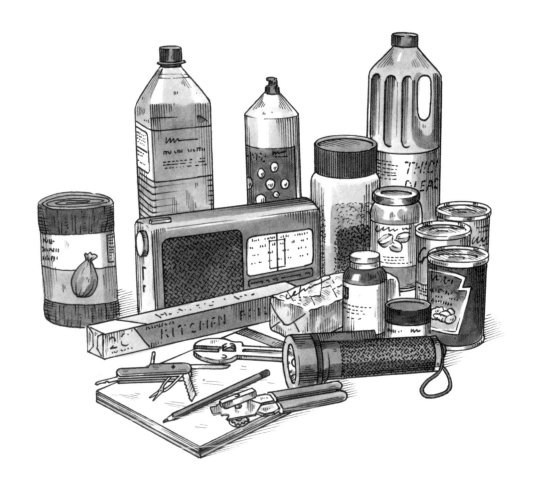

- Bottled water
- Medications
- Veterinary records
- Photo of your pet for identification purposes
- Cat litter and tray
- Food dishes

Livestock

Evacuate livestock whenever possible. Make advance arrangements for evacuation of livestock, including routes and host sites. The evacuation sites should have food, water, veterinary care and handling equipment. Appropriate vehicles for transporting livestock should be available along with experienced handlers to drive them. If you cannot evacuate your livestock, you must decide whether to move large animals to a barn or other available shelter or leave them outside. This decision should be based on how sturdy the shelter is and its location.

Emergency car kit

Keep this kit in the boot (trunk) of your car:

- Jumper cables
- First aid kit and manual
- Battery-powered radio, torch (flashlight) and extra batteries
- Blanket
- Small fire extinguisher
- Bottled water and non-perishable food items, such as muesli (granola) bars and raisins.
- Maps, shovel, flares
- Tyre (tire) repair kit and pump
- Umbrella
- Change for pay phone

Tools and Supplies

- Battery-powered radio
- Battery-powered torches (flashlights)
- Extra batteries
- Pocket (snap-blade) knife
- Matches in a waterproof bag
- Wrench (spanner) to turn off utilities
- Plastic bin (garbage) bags and ties
- Paper and pencil
- Household bleach

Flood watches and warnings

When authorities issue a flash flood watch take it very seriously. Be alert to signs of flooding and prepare to evacuate at a moment's notice. When a flash flood warning is issued or you realize flash flooding is imminent, act quickly. Do not hesitate to evacuate to higher ground. There may be only minutes or seconds before your home is inundated.

DURING A FLOOD

- Do not wait to evacuate if you see a flood approaching.
- Do not drive into areas that have been blocked off by authorities.
- Do not drive too close to storm drains or irrigation ditches.
- Do not drive through a flooded area. Turn your car around and find another route if you come upon a flooded road.
- If your car stalls, abandon it immediately and move to higher ground. It is better to watch your car being washed away than it is to be inside it while it's happening.
- Do not walk through flooded areas. As little as 15cm (6in) of moving water can knock you down.
- Avoid downed power lines. Water is an excellent conductor of electricity and electrocution is a major cause of death in floods.
- Watch out for snakes that may have taken shelter in your home.
- If rising waters have trapped you in your home, move upstairs, to the attic or, if necessary, onto the roof.
- Wait for rescuers to find you. Do not attempt to swim to safety.
- Place sandbags to block floodwaters.
- Lock your house.
- If outdoors, climb up to higher ground and stay there.

After a flood

Do not attempt to return to your home until authorities have indicated it is safe to do so.

- Check for injuries to yourself and others and apply first aid as needed.
- Inspect any damaged buildings before entering them to ensure serious structural damage has not occurred. Badly damaged buildings can collapse on you.
- If a door sticks at the top, it could mean the ceiling is on the verge of collapse. If you have to force open the door, wait

outside to see if any debris falls before entering.

- Once you enter the building, use a torch (flashlight). Do not use matches, lighters or any other type of flame because there may be gas trapped inside the building and an explosion could occur.
- Check the ceiling for signs of sagging. This could indicate imminent collapse.
- Check for gas leaks. If you do hear gas hissing or smell gas, open a window and get out of the building immediately. Turn off the gas at the main valve outside. Phone the gas supplier from a neighbour's house, cell phone or pay phone.
- Check for electrical system damage. If you see frayed wires or sparks, or if you smell hot insulation, turn off the electricity at the main circuit breaker or fuse box. Never stand in water while turning off electricity.
- Call your insurance agent as soon as possible to file a claim.
- Do not turn on the power until an electrician has declared your system safe.
- Until local authorities announce that your water supply is safe, boil all water for drinking or food preparation for at least five minutes.

- Be careful while walking around. Floodwaters are unsanitary and leave behind a variety of debris, including rusty nails and broken glass. There will also be lots of hazardous slippery mud.
- Clean up your home right away to rid it of the remnants of any sewage or chemicals the floodwaters might have washed in. Throw out foods and medicines that may have come into contact with the floodwaters.
- Do not allow children to play in floodwaters because it can hide hazards, such as broken glass, and it is unsanitary. Children can be swept into drains and drowned.
- Do not go sightseeing around disaster areas. Conditions there are dangerous and your presence could interfere with rescue or other emergency operations.

Experiencing a severe flood can be traumatic, especially if your home is damaged. In the wake of a flood, it is extremely important that you focus on maintaining your health and well being. Eat well and rest often. Don't over-exert yourself. Make a list of clean-up tasks and do them one at a time on a manageable schedule.

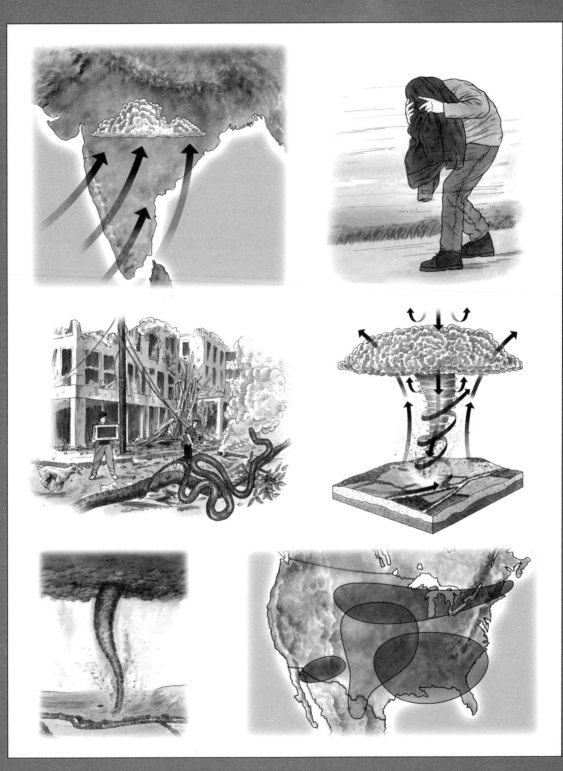

CHAPTER FIVE

High Winds

Mammoth hurricanes bring lashing rains and extensive flooding, lasting up to a week. The concentrated, devastating violence of a tornado can pass in minutes. Each year these storms kill thousands of people and destroy property. Knowing what course of action to take when these storms approach is key to survival.

People are both fascinated and terrified by the awesome, destructive force of hurricanes and tornadoes. Anyone who has experienced either of these weather phenomena will have a healthy respect for the devastation they wreak. Hurricanes leave widespread damage in their wake while the damage of a tornado as it suddenly dips down from the sky, leaving an entire community in ruins, tends to be more localized.

Improved forecasting capabilities and early warning systems have drastically decreased the number of deaths associated with hurricanes and tornadoes. The lack of commercial radio prior to the 1920s made it difficult to warn people spread over a large area of approaching storms. Now there are many sources of up-to-the-minute weather information that allow communities the benefit of advance warning.

Modern building codes have also increased survival chances. Before poured concrete foundations, homes merely sat on stone foundations and were not bolted down, rendering the home vulnerable to high winds. A wood-burning stove in a wind-damaged home could start a fire that would spread to other homes nearby.

While hurricane- and tornado-related fatalities have dramatically decreased since 1900, the cost of property damage has exponentially increased. This can be attributed to several factors: the nature of monetary inflation dictates that a home that incurs damage this year will be appraised as having a significantly higher value than that same home would have been appraised at 100 years ago. More people are building in marginal areas, such as beachfronts where hurricanes make landfall or in hills subject to mudslides. With the growth of the world's population, there are simply more structures to accommodate all the extra people. If there are more structures, more property damage is possible.

HURRICANES

A hurricane is a tropical storm characterized by winds with a constant speed of 120 kilometres (74 miles) per hour or greater rotating around a relatively calm centre known as the eye. It is the most destructive storm nature has to offer. These intense, rapidly rotating storm systems can produce sustained winds of 250 kilometres (150 miles) per hour with gusts of up to 300 kilometres (190 miles) per hour, bring enormous bands of heavy rains, create storm surges and spawn tornadoes. Hurricanes typically measure anywhere from 500 to 800 kilometres (300–500 miles) in diameter. Because hurricanes require warm water to fuel them, they occur when the sea's surface temperature reaches its warmest at about 26.6°C to 30°C (80°F–86°F). In the Northern Hemisphere, the hurricane season stretches from July to October with the peak occurring during the months of August and September. The Southern Hemisphere's hurricane season extends from November through April, with the peak season in the months of January and February.

Birth of a hurricane

The tropics provide the conditions necessary for the formation of a hurricane. In fact, hurricanes start out as tropical storms. Warm ocean water of at least 26.6°C (80°F), warm and moist air, and winds converging near the surface of the ocean feed these storms. Unstable air in the area allows winds to rise, which creates large areas of clouds. These clouds form clusters of thunderstorms. If these storms form more than six degrees north or south of the equator, the Coriolis effect causes them to rotate. Once it begins spinning, the storm system moves in a path away from the equator. Tropical storms normally do not travel more than 30° north or south of the equator because seawater is much cooler at these latitudes. If their path reverses and takes them towards the equator, the storm will lose its power because the Coriolis effect weakens as it nears the equator. The clusters of thunderstorms are formed into spiral bands by the spinning motion of the storm system. The bands of thunderstorms convert heat from the ocean into energy needed to continue its rotating motion. Aided by upper-level winds that spiral outwards and draw the rising air away from the developing storm, the intensity of its winds and speed of its rotation increase. When the winds reach a sustained speed of 120 kilometres (74 miles) per hour or greater, the storm is officially deemed a hurricane.

The eye, or centre, of the storm is comparatively calm and marks the area of lowest pressure. The most violent part of the storm takes place in the eyewall, or area immediately surrounding the eye. Though a mature hurricane contains hundreds of thunderstorms, it is in the eyewall that the strongest winds and most violent thunderstorms occur.

Coriolis effect

In 1835, Gustave-Gaspard de Coriolis observed that earth's rotation causes moving objects, such as ocean currents and winds, to be deflected from their original direction. The deflection is to the right along the direction of travel in the Northern Hemisphere, and to the left in the Southern Hemisphere. This effect is most pronounced at the poles. At the equator there is no deviation. The Coriolis effect causes air to rotate around high and low pressure centres and affects the direction of the rotation. Notably, they help give a hurricane its spin.

Tropical cyclone classification

The general term for all circulating weather systems over tropical waters is *tropical cyclone*. This term encompasses hurricanes, tropical storms, tropical depressions and tropical disturbances.

Comparison of cyclone, hurricane and tornado

Though cyclones, hurricanes, and tornadoes all have winds spiraling inwards towards a low pressure centre, they have significant differences. They differ in size, wind velocity, speed of travel, and duration.

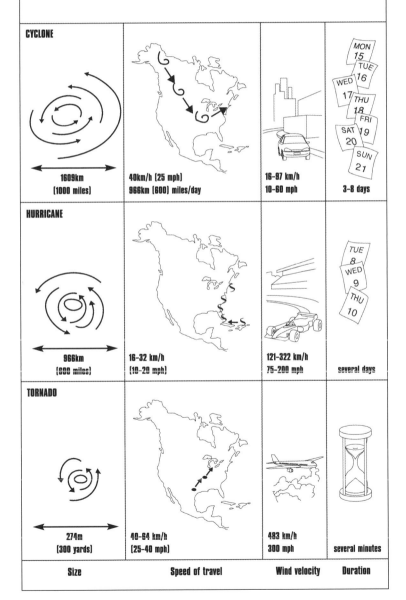

	Size	Speed of travel	Wind velocity	Duration
CYCLONE	1609km (1000 miles)	40km/h (25 mph) 966km (600) miles/day	16-97 km/h 10-60 mph	3-8 days
HURRICANE	966km (600 miles)	16-32 km/h (10-20 mph)	121-322 km/h 75-200 mph	several days
TORNADO	274m (300 yards)	40-64 km/h (25-40 mph)	483 km/h 300 mph	several minutes

Tropical disturbance: a low pressure area with rotating winds of 29 kilometres (18 miles) per hour or less.

Tropical depression: an organized system of clouds and thunderstorms with a defined circulation and maximum sustained winds of 60 kilometres (38 miles) per hour or less.

Tropical storm: an organized system of strong thunderstorms with a defined circulation and maximum sustained winds of 63 to 117 kilometres (39-73 miles) per hour.

Hurricane: an intense tropical weather system with a well defined circulation and maximum sustained winds of 119 kilometres (74 miles) per hour or higher.

(Source: NOAA)

Typhoons, cyclones and hurricanes

Typhoon, cyclone and hurricane are regional terms used to describe the same feature: a rotating tropical storm with maximum sustained winds of 119 kilometres (74 miles) per hour or higher. Which term is used is dependent upon where the storm originated. In the western Pacific and China Sea the word *typhoon* is used. In the Indian Ocean they are known as 'tropical

Occurence of typhoons, hurricanes and cyclones

Rotating tropical storms with maximum sustained winds of at least 119km (74 miles) per hour are known as typhoons, hurricanes, or cyclones. Which term is used to describe them depends upon where the storm originated.

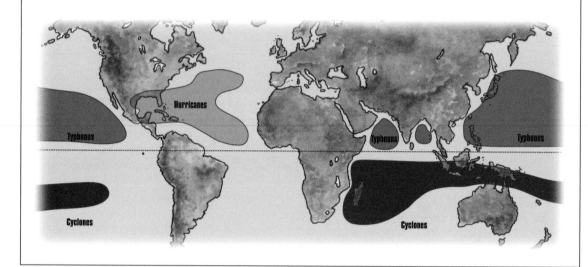

cyclones'. In North America the term *hurricane* is used.

Storm surge

More deaths are caused by storm surge than by a hurricane's violent winds and torrential rains. Meteorologists describe the storm surge as the difference between the actual storm tide and what would have been normal tide had there been no storm. Surface water is drawn upwards into the hurricane's low-pressure centre as it passes over the ocean. The result is a mound of water that rises about 30.5cm (1ft) higher than the surrounding ocean surface. In stronger hurricanes this wall of water can measure 80 to 160 kilometres (50-100 miles) wide and more than 3m (10ft) high where it makes landfall. Along the coast, storm surge is the most immediate threat to life and property.

Wind speeds decrease fairly rapidly as a hurricane moves over land, but flooding is still a danger. Torrential rains in combination with the storm surge inundate the land in a short space of time with more precipitation than it can absorb.

Survivor's story

In 1992, writer k.t. Frankovich and her son were taken by surprise by the destructive force of Hurricane Andrew in Florida.

'South Dade had not been advised to evacuate or seek shelter the night Andrew struck. We had been reassured by the news media that Andrew would strike around the Palm Beach–North Lauderdale area. We were told to expect 50-mile [80-kilometre] per hour winds and rain but that was it.

The majority of South Dade residents were in bed sleeping when Andrew's 214-mile [343-kilometre] per hour winds suddenly slammed into us like a gigantic killer tornado. But unlike a killer tornado that passes by within seconds, Hurricane Andrew stayed on top of us for over six-and-a-half hours, with no let up. How well I remember the horrible sound of those winds coming at us like a speeding locomotive from hell. So fierce, once the first wall of winds plowed into us it sounded like we had been sucked into a monstrous revved-up jet engine.

My terrified son and I were in a small manufactured apartment commonly referred to as a pre-fab apartment. Actually, a pre-fab apartment is nothing more than a glorified trailer without the trailer hitch. Our entire building was about the size of a double-width trailer and had been built to withstand 100-mile [160-kilometre] per hour winds, nothing higher. The very instant the first wall of winds slammed into us, the entire building began to shake apart. I remember feeling like I was trapped in a tornado and earthquake happening at the same time.

Our apartment exploded apart when a two-story concrete transformer pole, carrying electrical lines, torpedoed right through our living room wall, directly in the path of where I stood paralyzed in fear. I will never forget the horrifying sight as long as I live. Upon impact, the entire building ruptured in a massive explosion, hurling speeding roof beams from all directions. I was struck

in the head three separate times. The impact was so fierce that my jaw was broken and I lost eight teeth, along with the optic nerve to each of my eyes being severely damaged ... to the point that it would inevitably cause me to go blind.

My son and I spent the entire night struggling to survive moment by moment. Without anything to protect us from the voracious jaws of Andrew, it was nothing short of a miracle that we weren't sucked up by the winds and pitched out into the storm so like many who lost their lives that horrible night. Or that we weren't killed by the flying debris hurled on top of us.'

SURVIVING A HURRICANE
Before the Hurricane

- Take steps to protect your home from high winds and flooding (as discussed earlier).
- Purchase flood insurance. Homeowners insurance does not cover flood damage.
- Agree on a place inland where your family can go in case evacuation is necessary. This can be the home of a friend or relative, a shelter or a motel away from the coast.
- Plan an evacuation route based on routes inland that are known to be safe or are designated as evacuation routes. Be prepared to drive 30 to 80 kilometres (20–50 miles) inland to find a safe place.

Saffir-Simpson Hurricane Scale

Scale Number (Category)	Sustained Winds (kph [mph])	Storm Surge (m [ft])	Damage
1	118–152 (74–95)	1.2–1.6 (4–5)	Minimal
2	153–176 (96–110)	1.7–2.5 (6–8)	Moderate
3	177–208 (111–130)	2.6–3.7 (9–12)	Extensive
4	209–248 (131–155)	3.8–5.4 (13–18)	Extreme
5	Greater than 248 (> 155)	Greater than 5.4 (>18)	Catastrophic

- Get a current road map of your area. You may have to plan an alternate route if normal evacuation routes are clogged with traffic.
- Ask a friend who lives outside of the storm area to agree to be a family contact. It is often easier to make a long distance call after a hurricane. Be sure that everyone in the family knows the contact's name, address and phone number.

This will help family members reunite if they are separated during the hurricane.
- Store emergency supplies where they can be retrieved easily.
- Make sure every member of your household knows how to respond to a hurricane.
- Teach everyone in the family how and when to turn off the gas, electricity and water.

Anatomy of a hurricane

The center of relative calm in a hurricane is known as the eye. Many bands of thunderstorms, called rain bands, spiral inwards towards the eye. The fastest winds occur in the eyewall where gusts to 300km/h (185mph) have been measured. These dangerous storms can measure as large as 483km (300 miles) in diameter and tower as high as 18,000m (60,000ft).

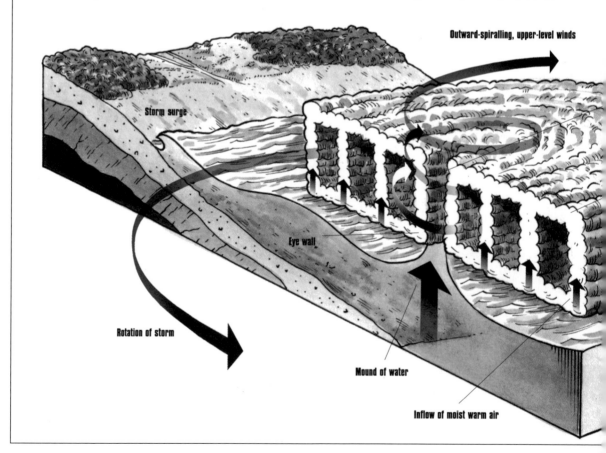

Outward-spiralling, upper-level winds

Storm surge

Eye wall

Rotation of storm

Mound of water

Inflow of moist warm air

- If you do not have storm shutters, protect your windows with a criss-cross pattern of masking tape. This will cut down on the amount of flying glass should your windows be broken by the storm.
- If they are not tied down securely, store rubbish bins (garbage cans), garden tools, lawn furniture and any grills indoors. Lock up bicycles.
- If you are in a low-lying area, move to higher ground.
- If you are in a boat, get to shore, secure the boat and seek shelter.
- Fill the tank of your car with fuel.
- Listen to the radio for weather updates and instructions from authorities.
- If you are instructed by authorities to evacuate, do so with haste. More people tend to hesitate and drag their feet than panic when faced with severe weather.
- If you evacuate, take pets with you.

EMERGENCY SUPPLIES
Water
It helps to keep 13.5 litres (3 gallons) of water on hand for each member of your household. Store the water in clean plastic containers. Replace it with fresh water every six months. If you are caught without a supply of clean drinking water, you can melt ice cubes or use the water in your hot water tank. As a last resort, use the water in your toilet tank. Do not use the water in the toilet bowl.

If none of those emergency water sources are available, you can purify contaminated water by boiling it for five minutes. Or you can add sixteen drops of household bleach per 4.5 litres (gallon) of water, stir, and let it stand for 30 minutes.

Food
Because utility service may be interrupted after a hurricane, store at least a three-day supply of non-perishable food. Choose foods that need no cooking, refrigeration, or preparation. Rotate food items once a year.

- Tinned juices, milk, and soup
- High energy foods such as peanut butter, muesli (granola) bars, dried fruit and nuts mix, biscuits
- Ready-to-eat tinned meats, fruits and vegetables
- Vitamins

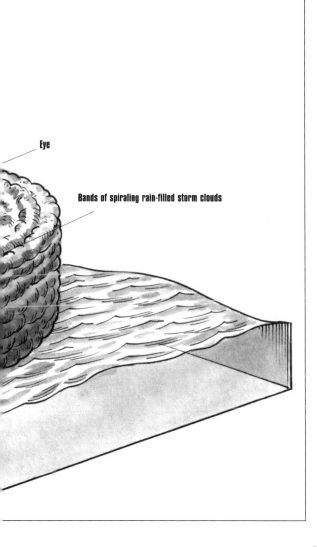

Eye

Bands of spiraling rain-filled storm clouds

Paths of tropical cyclones

Hurricane season runs from July to October in the Northern Hemisphere and from November to April in the Southern Hemisphere.

Tropical cyclones require very warm sea surface temperatures to form. These are the paths tropical cyclones typically take.

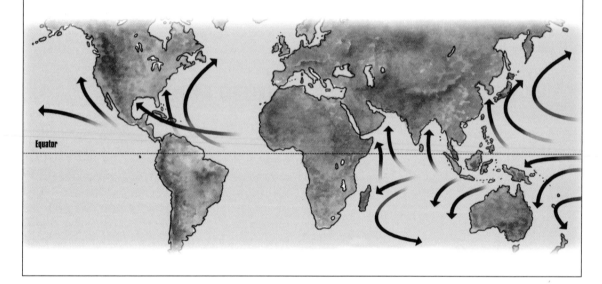

Equator

- Special foods that infants or the elderly might require
- Biscuits (cookies), boiled sweets (hard candy), sweetened cereal, raisins, chocolate, tea bags, instant coffee
- Manual can opener
- Paper plates, plastic cups and cutlery, or camping mess kits
- Washing up liquid (liquid detergent)
- Aluminium foil and paper kitchen towels or toilet paper
- Non-perishable pet food

First Aid Kit
- Various sizes of adhesive bandages
- Various sizes of sterile gauze pads
- Adhesive tape
- Triangular bandages
- Sterile rolled bandages
- Cotton wool and swabs
- Scissors

- Tweezers
- Sewing needle
- Antiseptic
- Iodine
- Thermometer
- Soap
- Assorted sizes of safety pins
- Moist wipes
- Rubber (latex) gloves
- Sun block
- Insect repellent
- Aspirin or other pain reliever
- Prescription medications
- Anti-diarrhoea medicine
- Laxative
- Antacid

Clothes and personal items
- A change of clothing, sturdy shoes, rain gear
- Blankets or sleeping bags

- Extra set of car keys
- Toilet paper
- Toiletry and personal hygiene items
- Extra pair of glasses or contact lenses and supplies
- Credit cards and cash
- Books
- Toys for children

Emergency car kit
Keep this kit in the boot (trunk) of your car:
- Jumper cables
- First aid kit and manual
- Battery-powered radio, torch (flashlight) and extra batteries
- Blanket
- Small fire extinguisher
- Bottled water and non-perishable food items, such as muesli (granola) bars
- Maps, shovel, flares

- Tyre (tire) repair kit and pump
- Umbrella
- Change for pay phone

Tools and Supplies
- Battery-powered radio
- Battery-powered torches (flashlights)
- Extra batteries
- Pocket (snap-blade) knife
- Matches in a waterproof bag
- Wrench (spanner) to turn off utilities
- Plastic bin (garbage) bags and ties
- Paper and pencil
- Household bleach

Caravans (mobile homes)
Caravans (mobile homes) are not built to withstand hurricane-force winds. Secure your caravan (mobile home) to a foundation or anchor it with over-the-top or frame ties.

Monsoon areas of the world

The most powerful monsoons occur in southern Asia, Africa, and northern Australia. These seasonal winds bring widespread torrential rain and flooding, and often are very disruptive. However, the monsoons are not necessarily dreaded; about half the world's population relies on the monsoon rains to replenish water supplies.

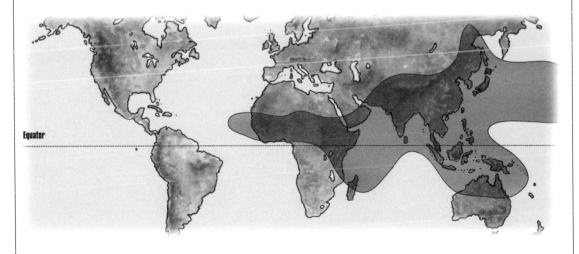

Equator

When a hurricane warning is issued, do what you can to secure your valuables, then evacuate and take refuge at a shelter or with friends or relatives.

- Install shutters on all windows.
- Take down mirrors and tape them. Wrap your mirrors and lamps in blankets and put them in the bathtub or shower.

Summer monsoon

India experiences the most dramatic monsoon winds. In summer, a low pressure area develops over the Tibetan Plateau's hot interior. Warm, moist air is drawn inland from the Indian Ocean, and heavy rains result. Even more rain is produced when the moist air reaches the Himalayas and is forced upwards by the mountain range.

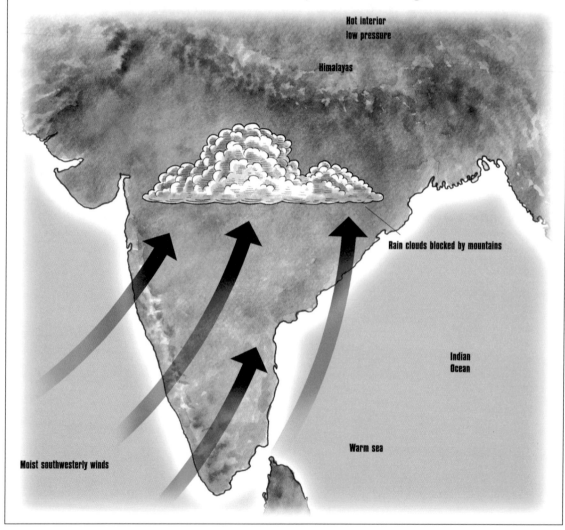

Hot interior
low pressure

Himalayas

Rain clouds blocked by mountains

Indian
Ocean

Warm sea

Moist southwesterly winds

Protecting caravans (mobile homes)

- Pack breakables in boxes and place the boxes on the floor.
- Store lawn furniture, awnings, rubbish bins (garbage cans) and other loose outdoor objects.
- Disconnect electricity, sewer and water lines. Shut off propane tanks and anchor them securely to the ground.

Watches and warnings

Tropical Storm Watch: tropical storm conditions are possible, usually within 36 hours.

Tropical Storm Warning: tropical storm conditions are expected, usually within 24 hours.

Hurricane Watch: hurricane conditions are possible, usually within 36 hours.

Hurricane Warning: hurricane conditions are expected, usually within 24 hours.

Short-term Watches and Warnings: provide detailed information on specific hurricane threats, such as tornadoes, floods and high winds

Pets

- If you evacuate your home, do not leave pets behind. Even if they do survive the storm, they may be frightened enough to run away.
- Be sure that identification tags have current information and are securely attached to your pet's collar.
- Have a secure pet carrier, lead (leash) or harness for your pet so if he panics, he can't run away.
- Keep a current photo of your pet in case he gets lost.
- Never ever leave your pet chained outside during a storm.
- Pack a pet survival kit in advance.

- Many emergency shelters do not allow pets. Find out well in advance which hotels allow pets.
- If there is absolutely no alternative but leaving your pet at home when you evacuate, confine your pet to a safe area indoors. Select an easily cleaned area, such as a utility room or bathroom. Do not choose a room with windows. The room should have counters to provide higher ground for the pet in case water rises in the room. Establish two separate rooms if you have dogs and cats. Put a note on the front door indicating what pets are in the house and where they are located. Write your contact number and the number of the vet who looks after your pet on the note.

Pet Survival Kit

- Non-perishable pet food
- Bottled water
- Medications
- Vet records
- Photo of your pet for identification purposes
- Cat litter and tray
- Food dishes

Livestock

It is best to evacuate livestock whenever possible. Make advance arrangements for evacuation of livestock, including routes and host sites. The evacuation sites should have food, water, vet care and handling equipment. Appropriate vehicles for transporting livestock should be available along with experienced handlers to drive them. If you cannot evacuate your livestock, you must decide whether to move large animals to a barn or other available shelter or leave them outside. This decision should be based on how sturdy the shelter is and its location.

During the hurricane

- Stay indoors, away from windows, skylights and glass doors.

Winter monsoon

In winter the sun is lower in the sky. The air over the Tibetan Plateau cools, producing a high pressure area. This area results in monsoon winds that blow across India and out to sea. These winds keep moist air over the ocean, creating clear skies over India.

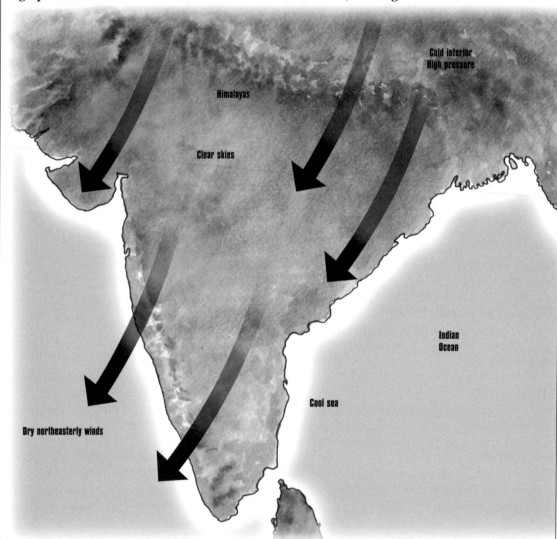

Cold interior
High pressure

Himalayas

Clear skies

Indian
Ocean

Cool sea

Dry northeasterly winds

- If you have a basement or storm cellar, go there to wait out the storm.
- If you do not have a basement or storm cellar, remain on the lowest floor of your home until the hurricane has subsided.
- Do not use candles to light your home if the power fails. Many fires begin from candles. Use torches (flashlights).
- Unplug small appliances. This includes the television.

- Turn the refrigerator to its coldest setting and open it only when necessary.
- Listen to a battery-powered radio for reports on the storm's progress.
- Avoid lifts (elevators). The power can go out and you could be trapped.
- Close all interior doors.
- Be alert for tornadoes that may form.
- If you are in a car, seek shelter. Do not drive into floodwaters. If you come upon a flooded road, turn around and go another way.
- Do not be fooled into thinking the storm is over when the eye passes over. The worst part of the storm will happen once the eye passes and winds blow from the opposite direction. The calm of the eye can last anywhere from two minutes to half an hour.
- Remain calm. The storm will pass.

After the hurricane

- Stay tuned to local radio for word from authorities about whether it is safe to return to your home.
- Wear sturdy shoes.
- Assist any injured or trapped people. Administer first aid where needed.
- Avoid fallen power lines and report them immediately to the power company or emergency services.
- Report broken sewers or water mains to the utility company.
- Inspect your home for any possible structural damage before entering it.
- Beware of snakes, insects and other dangerous animals driven to higher ground by floodwaters. They may have sought refuge in your home.
- Once you re-enter your home, use a torch (flashlight). Do not use matches, lighters or any other type of flame. There may be gas trapped inside the building and an explosion could occur.
- Open windows and doors to ventilate and dry your home.

- Throw out any food that has spoiled or come into contact with floodwaters.
- Restrict telephone use to emergency calls only.
- Drive only if absolutely necessary and avoid flooded roads.
- Check for gas leaks. If you do hear gas hissing or smell gas, open a window and get out of the building immediately. Turn off the gas at the main valve outside and phone the gas supplier from a neighbour's house, mobile (cell) phone or pay phone.
- Check for electrical system damage. If you see frayed wires or sparks, or if you smell hot insulation, turn off the electricity at the main circuit breaker or fuse box. Never stand in water while turning off electricity.
- Call your insurance agent as soon as possible to file a claim.
- Until local authorities announce that your water supply is safe, boil all water for drinking or food preparation for at least five minutes.
- Be extremely careful if using a chainsaw to cut fallen trees.
- Take photographs of any damage to your home for insurance purposes.

TORNADOES

A tornado is a funnel-shaped vortex of air extending from the base of a cumulonimbus cloud to the ground. A centre of low pressure surrounds this violently whirling air that mangles everything in its path. Advancing across the landscape at an average of 50 kilometres (30 miles) per hour, some of the strongest tornadoes have winds of more than 400 kilometres (250 miles) per hour. Tornadoes can occur at any time of year and have appeared on every continent except Antarctica. Although most tornadoes occur between 4 p.m. and 9 p.m., they can strike at any hour if conditions are right. Many of them last only a few minutes and damage

Post storm hazards

In the aftermath of a tornado or hurricane, storm-damaged buildings can be structurally unsound and collapse. Damaged utility lines or mains present fire and electrocution hazards.

Normally docile pets may become disoriented and aggressive. Snakes are driven to higher ground by flood waters that accompany storms. Beware of looters who may be armed.

narrow sections of land, but more severe ones can last an hour and wreak havoc for a distance of 96 kilometres (60 miles). Tornadoes can occur as a single vortex or as an outbreak where multiple twisters form.

How a tornado forms

In the upper levels of a storm, high-speed winds cause rotation. The spiralling updraught (updraft) of air in the storm fuels the storm. A spinning column of air descends through the updraught (updraft) area and emerges through the cloud base. As this spinning column of air reaches the ground, a tornado is formed.

Tornadoes strike suddenly, leaving little time to prepare for them. These are warning signs that tornado survivors have described:

● A strange quiet that occurs during or shortly after a thunderstorm.

- Debris falling from the sky.
- Clouds passing by rapidly, especially in a rotating pattern.
- A sickly greenish or greenish-black colour to the sky.
- A sound like rushing air that changes to a roar.
- An approaching cloud of debris without a visible funnel.

Tornado myths

1. *Tornadoes are always visible from a great distance.*

They can be hidden in heavy rainfall.

2. *Tornadoes never strike big cities.*

Miami and St Louis have both experienced tornadoes.

3. *Tornadoes cause houses to explode from changes in air pressure.*

Houses are damaged by strong winds and debris not changes in air pressure. When debris breaks windows, winds get inside and push upwards on the roof and outwards on the walls. Winds as low as 96 kilometres (60 miles) per hour can lift off a roof that isn't properly attached. Once the roof is ripped away, the walls fall outwards, making the house appear as though it has exploded.

4. *By opening the windows, you can balance the pressure inside and outside your house so a tornado will not do damage.*

The force of a tornado can rip through a struc-ture, whether the windows are open or not. Even with the windows closed most houses have enough openings to vent the pressure difference in the time it takes a tornado to pass.

5. *The best place to be during a tornado is generally in the southwest corner of the basement.*

This used to be a safety rule based on the idea that debris would usually not be deposited there, however there is no concrete evidence to back up this theory .The current best advice is to move to a protected interior room on the lowest floor of the building, as far as possible from exterior walls and windows.

Tornado alley

The United States has the most intense tornadoes in the world. With about a thousand touching down each year, it also has the greatest number.

A majority of these tornadoes happen in Tornado Alley, an area that extends across northern Texas, Oklahoma, Kansas, and southern Nebraska.

Fujita Scale

Scale Number	Wind Speed (kph [mph])	Amount of Damage	Type of Damage
F0	64–117 (40–73)	Light	Chimney damage, tree branches broken
F1	118–180 (74–112)	Moderate	Mobile homes pushed off foundation or overturned
F2	181–251 (113–157)	Considerable	Mobile homes demolished, trees uprooted
F3	252–330 (158–206)	Severe	Roofs and walls torn down, trains overturned, cars thrown
F4	331–417 (207–260)	Devastating	Well constructed walls levelled
F5	Greater than 418 (> 261)	Incredible	Homes lifted off foundations and carried considerable distances

6. *Motorway flyovers (highway overpasses) are a safe place to seek shelter under if you are driving when you spot a tornado.*

People have been killed when seeking shelter under flyovers (overpasses). If the tornado strikes the flyover (overpass), you will not be protected.

7. *Tornadoes cannot cross water.*

A waterspout is a type of tornado that actually forms on water, and tornadoes that form on land can cross bodies of water such as rivers and lakes.

8. *Areas near lakes rivers, and mountains are safe from tornadoes.*

Tornadoes can climb up and down hillsides. One tornado near Yellowstone National Park left a path of destruction along the slopes of a 3050-m (10,000-ft) mountain.

9. *A tornado is always accompanied or preceded by a funnel cloud.*

Especially in the early stages, a tornado can be causing damage on the ground even though a visible funnel cloud is not present. Likewise, if you see a funnel cloud but it does not appear to be 'touching down', a tornadic circulation may nonetheless be in contact with the ground.

10. *Downward-bulging clouds mean tornadoes are on the way.*

This may be the case, especially with those which show evidence of a rotating motion, but many of these clouds are not associated with tornadoes and may be completely harmless.

Waterspouts

Waterspouts look like tornadoes over water, but they are not associated with thunderstorms. Generally they are much less intense than tornadoes. When winds rotating near the water's surface interact with the updraught (updraft) of a cumulus cloud, the result is a waterspout. A tornadic waterspout occurs when a fully developed tornado moves out over the water, sucking up water and raining down fish.

Survivors' stories

On 18 March 1925, tornadoes killed 689 people in Missouri, Illinois and Indiana. The event is referred to as the Tri-State Tornado. This is Alice Jones Schedler's account of what happened to her family and home.

'Dad said, "Grab the two little ones and let's get to a ditch. I just saw a house about

Waterspouts

Waterspouts are rapidly rotating columns of air that form over warm oceans and lakes. Variations in wind near the water's surface cause updrafts. Moist air rotating in the vortex cools as it rises, and the condensing water droplets make the whirling wind visible.

Distended cloud base

Funnel

Spray

a mile away blown up into bits."

Then our swing on the porch came through the front window and we were all out for a while.

I came to and started crawling around a lot of bricks - what had been the chimney. Dad hollered at me and asked if I could get up and walk. He took me by the hand and led me outside to where Mom and the two little ones were sitting on the ground. He said, 'I'll go find the two older boys' - as he said this, he was walking up the side of a wall leaning on the kitchen table.

My brother Winnis was on the table with the whole wall on him mashing the breath out of him by inches.

My dad screamed for help to different people in the street. No one came so he told me to help him get the wall up off Winnis. He with God's help did the impossible and raised the wall 2 to 3 inches [5-8cm], enough so I could help Winnis to the floor. Later they came back and said it couldn't be lifted by one man, but he did it.

My other older brother, Roger, flew with the back door two blocks to the school-

When tornadoes are most likely to occur

Though tornadoes can occur at any time of the year, they are more likely at certain times in certain regions. There is an overall peak in activity from April to June in tornado alley. The Gulf states experience most of their tornadoes in the winter.

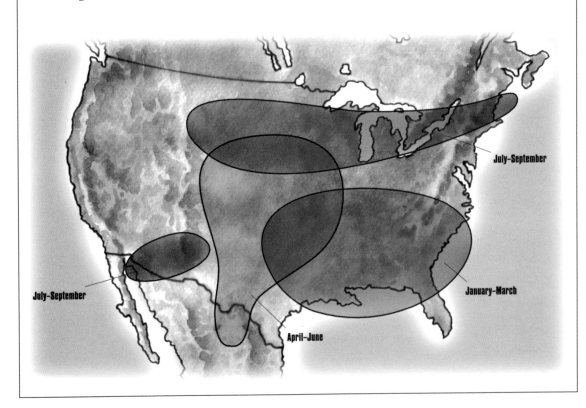

July-September

July-September

January-March

April-June

house. He came walking home by himself, a complete mess of blood from big cuts on his head and shoulders. He walked like a zombie, one small step at a time.

Then it rained and hailed so we were soaked.

Dad's brother Henry Jones lived one house away so Dad told us to follow him and to step only where he did because of fallen wires. They had three rooms left upstairs and put the little ones in bed and the ambulance came and took two brothers to the hospital. Both Roger and Winnis survived.

But I saw one of our neighbours, Mr Hubbard, laying with a table leg through his body. Mom kept saying, "Don't look, don't look.'"

Alice's brother Winnis Jones gives his own account of being trapped beneath the wall:

"I and three of my friends were playing marbles near my home. It got so dark we had to go inside. It was about eighteen minutes after four. Dad had just entered the house. That made nine people in our large

Lying flat in a ditch

If caught outdoors during a tornado, lie flat in a ditch or other low-lying area. Covering your head with your hands can help protect against flying debris. Most of the fatalities and injuries incurred during tornadoes are caused by flying debris.

The classic tornado profile

The image of the tapered funnel reaching 305m (1000ft) from the cloud to the ground is what most people imagine when tornadoes are mentioned. The truth is, tornadoes take on a variety of shapes. They can be shaped like bowls, cylinders, hourglasses, wedges, or ropes. All of them, regardless of shape, are dangerous.

I saw the storm topple a house and barn down a small hill a mile away. Then a brick or rock came through the window. The west wall came down, forcing me down on the table-top. All five legs (about 4in [10cm] or so in thickness) were broken and the table was lying on the floor. It would be impossible to describe the noise under this wall. You see, all gravel, coal, bricks, tin cans, bottles, fence posts and other debris was picked up by the storm's suction action. It beat against the wall like a huge drum.

Just a second or two and the tornado was gone. I heard voices above me asking where everyone was. My dad was looking for me. I could not speak, scream or make any noise because I knew if I did, I would be dead. I had just one breath, and the weight of the wall was so heavy, if I released it I would be dead. My dad in searching for me walked up on the wall. That almost did it for me. He finally saw part of my leg sticking out and he started to pry and lift the wall off of me. It was a really close call. My chest hurt real bad and I could just barely breathe.

country kitchen, including two neighbour boys. I was looking out of a door glass on a side porch. I saw the tornado coming about a mile away. I just had time to warn everybody in the house when it struck. It came with a noise like two freight trains.

All the family made it over to my uncle's house, which was not damaged too badly. There I was taken by ambulance to the hospital. I was there about ten days.'

The debris cloud

The first sign of a tornado's contact with the ground is a swirling cloud of dust and debris. This debris can include rocks, uprooted trees and other potentially dangerous items. Clouds, hills, trees, or heavy rain can hide the debris cloud from view.

SURVIVING TORNADOES
Before a Tornado

- Take steps to protect your home from high winds (as discussed earlier).
- Make sure each member of your household understands the difference between a tornado watch and tornado warning.
- Designate an area in your home as a shelter. Perform drills so family members will be accustomed to taking refuge in that area.
- Have a plan for reuniting in case family members are separated.
- Ask a friend or relative who lives outside of the storm area to agree to be a family contact. It is often easier to make a long distance call after a tornado. Be sure that everyone in the family knows the contact's name, address and phone number.
- Monitor television or radio newscasts.
- Have emergency supplies on hand.
- Know where public shelters are located.
- Fill your car's tank with fuel.
- Contain pets and livestock.
- If they are not tied down securely, store rubbish bins (garbage cans), lawn furniture and grills indoors.
- Prepare to evacuate or seek shelter in a storm cellar.

Covering head to protect against flying debris

The best place to be during high winds is inside. If you are caught making your way home when the wind picks up cover your head to protect yourself from flying debris and lean forward as you walk to make yourself smaller and to stop yourself from being blown over. If the wind becomes too strong to continue, lie flat on your front in a ditch or other low-lying area.

Emergency Supplies
- Torch (flashlight)
- Battery-powered radio
- Extra batteries
- First aid kit and manual
- Emergency food and water
- Manual can opener
- Prescription medicines

- Cash and credit cards
- Sturdy shoes

For a more comprehensive list of emergency supplies, consult the section on surviving hurricanes earlier in this chapter.

Ideal conditions for tornadoes

When warm, humid air from the Gulf of Mexico collided with the cold, dry air coming in from the Rockies and the cool, humid air from the Great Lakes in early April of 1974 there was a dramatic result. These are the conditions led to the Super Outbreak of 127 tornadoes, the strongest tornado outbreak ever recorded.

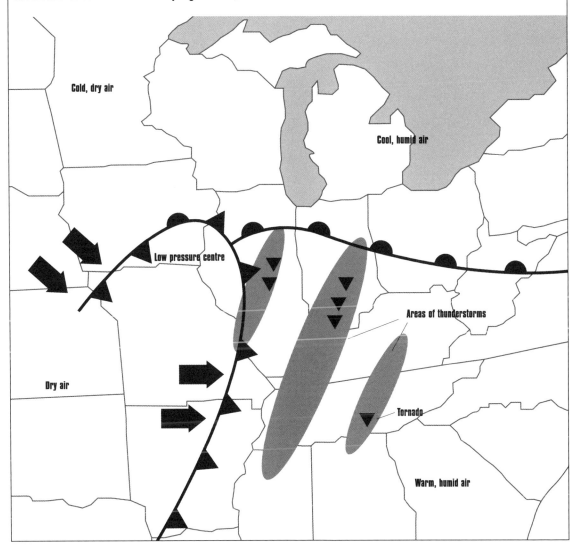

Pets

Do not abandon your pets during a tornado. Take them with you to safety. After a tornado passes familiar smells and landmarks can be missing and this could confuse your pet. Keep your pet on a lead (leash) so he does not panic and try to run away. For a list of emergency pet supplies, check the section on surviving hurricanes earlier in this chapter.

Caravans (mobile homes)

A caravan (mobile home) is the most dangerous place to be during a tornado. Most tornado deaths occur in cars and caravans (mobile homes). Know where the nearest shelter is located before a tornado strikes. Evacuate to that shelter and do not try to ride out a tornado in your caravan (mobile home). You are literally safer lying flat outside in a ditch than you are in a caravan (mobile home). An F1 tornado can push a caravan (mobile home) off of its foundation. Caravans disintegrate under the forces of an F2 tornado. These structures were simply not designed to withstand high winds.

Watches/Warnings

Tornado watch: issued when conditions are favourable for tornadoes over a wide area.

Tornado warning: issued when a tornado has been spotted locally or detected by radar.

Before a tornado

- The most dangerous part of a tornado is the flying debris. Dishes, broken glass, branches, nails, wood, furniture, curtain rods, and bricks can be transformed into lethal projectiles by tornadic winds. If you live in a tornado-prone area make a habit of securing any loose items.
- The direction your home faces contributes to the amount of damage it can sustain during a tornado. The most severe

tornadoes often approach from the west. Structural features such as garages, gables or porches that face west are most vulnerable. Be certain these features on your home are structurally sound and reinforced against high winds.

During a tornado

- If you have a basement or storm cellar, go there and wait for the tornado to pass.
- If your basement is not partitioned, go to its centre or under a stairwell. Corners tend to attract debris.
- If you do not have a basement or storm cellar, stay on the ground floor of your home.
- Seek refuge in a windowless interior room of your home.
- If you are in a wheelchair, set the brake and cover your head with a jacket or blanket.
- If you are in a building with a large, free-standing roof, such as an auditorium or gymnasium, seek safer shelter. The roof could easily collapse or be blown away.
- If you are outside, get indoors quickly.
- If you are outside and there is no shelter nearby, lie flat in a ditch, ravine or depression.
- If you are in a vehicle, get out and seek shelter immediately in a ditch or low-lying area away from the vehicle. Do not try to outrun a tornado.
- Remain calm.

After a tornado

- Assist trapped or injured people. Administer first aid where necessary.
- Avoid fallen power lines. Report them to the electric company or emergency services (police or fire department) as soon as possible.
- Restrict telephone use for emergency calls only.
- Evacuate your home immediately if you smell gas or hear the hissing sound of a

Anatomy of a tornado

Warm air flowing into the base of a cloud spirals upwards because of varying wind speed and direction. A spinning column of air, called the funnel, forms at the cloud's base.

Cold downdrafts from the cloud's upper layers descend. Though they last only a few minutes, the damage they cause can be devastating.

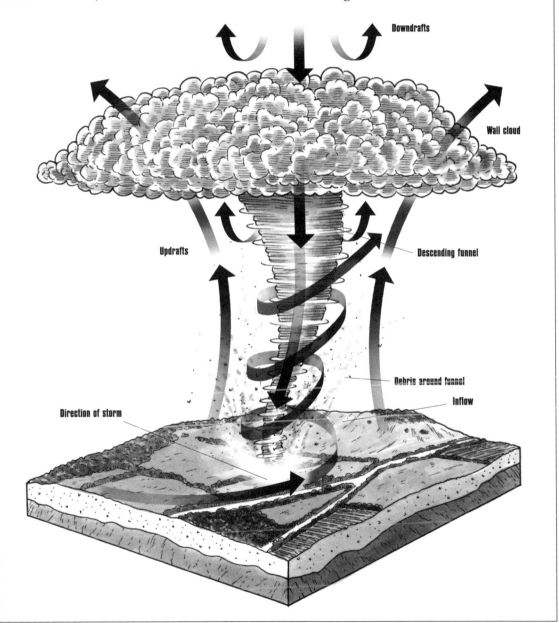

Downdrafts

Wall cloud

Updrafts

Descending funnel

Debris around funnel

Inflow

Direction of storm

Funnel cloud

An early indicator a tornado is brewing is the formation of a funnel cloud. The funnel extends from the dark base of a storm cloud.

Its tapered shape and smooth sides are easily recognizable as it descends and touches down as a tornado.

leaking gas pipe.

- Inspect any damaged buildings before entering them to ensure serious structural damage has not occurred. Badly damaged buildings can collapse on you.
- If a door sticks at the top, it could mean that the ceiling is on the verge of collapse. If you have to force open the door, wait outside to see if any debris falls before entering.
- Once you enter the building, use a torch (flashlight). Do not use matches, lighters or any other type of flame. There may be gas trapped inside the building and an explosion could occur.
- Check the ceiling for signs of sagging. This could indicate imminent collapse.
- If your home has not been damaged, keep children and pets inside.
- Avoid driving anywhere unless it is absolutely necessary. If you must drive, proceed with extreme caution. Roads may be littered with hazardous debris.
- Do not go sightseeing around disaster areas. Conditions there are dangerous and your presence could interfere with rescue or other emergency operations.

- Wear protective clothing and sturdy shoes while cleaning up.
- Clean spilled medicines, bleaches, petrol (gasoline) or other flammable liquids immediately.
- Do not despair. If your home is damaged, it can be rebuilt.

Cleanup

If assisting with cleanup efforts in the aftermath of a tornado, there are a number of items you can bring to help the victims and volunteers:

- Food and drink
- Tarps
- Plywood
- Tools and nails
- Garbage bags
- Boxes and packing materials
- Multiple pairs of heavy work gloves
- Masking tape
- Pens
- Cleaning supplies
- Lumbering tools
- Ladders
- Moving trucks

CHAPTER SIX

Extreme Cold

The human body functions optimally within a narrow range of temperature. Frostbite can lead to gangrene and amputation and extreme cold can be fatal. To survive the cold you must maintain a safe body temperature, avoid cold injuries, find shelter, and prepare your home and vehicle.

Whether you are in a city or the wilderness, extreme cold can be deadly. It is important that you stay warm and avoid any actions that can cause a rapid loss of body heat.

COLD AND THE HUMAN BODY

Normal core temperature for the human body is 37°C (98.6°F). In order to remain healthy this core temperature must stay constant within a narrow margin. Variations in either direction can cause irreparable organ damage and death.

Core temperature refers to the temperature of vital internal organs, including the heart, lungs and brain. Since the limbs and extremities have less protective tissue than the torso, their temperature tends to vary to a greater extent. It is important to keep the hands and feet warm to guard against heat loss and injury.

Shivering is the body's way of producing heat, yet prolonged shivering causes fatigue, which results in a drop in body temperature. To survive in a cold environment you must take care of your basic needs of food, water and shelter, as well as protect yourself from illness.

Wind chill

Wind accelerates heat loss and chills a person by carrying away body heat. Wind chill is a measurement of how wind and cold feel on exposed skin rather than a measure of the actual air temperature. Animals are also affected by wind chill, but plants and inanimate objects are not. Be aware that when wind is present, the temperature your body perceives is colder than what the thermometer reads.

COLD WEATHER CLOTHING

There are many ways to lose body heat in cold environments. To avoid heat loss

Wind Chill

Speed	Temperature °F							Speed	Temperature °C						
calm	25	15	5	0	-5	-15	-25	calm	-4	-9	-15	-18	-20	-26	-32
	Equivalent Chill Temperature (°F)								Equivalent Chill Temperature (°C)						
5 mph	22	11	0	-5	-10	-21	-31	8 kph	-6	-12	-18	-21	-23	-29	-35
10 mph	10	-3	-15	-22	-27	-40	-52	16 kph	-12	-19	-26	-30	-33	-40	-47
15 mph	2	-11	-25	-31	-38	-51	-65	24 kph	-17	-24	-32	-35	-39	-46	-54
20 mph	-3	-17	-31	-39	-46	-60	-74	32 kph	-19	-27	-35	-39	-43	-51	-59
25 mph	-7	-22	-36	-44	-51	-66	-81	40 kph	-21	-30	-38	-42	-46	-54	-63
30 mph	-10	-25	-41	-49	-56	-71	-86	48 kph	-23	-31	-41	-45	-48	-57	-65
35 mph	-12	-27	-43	-52	-58	-74	-89	56 kph	-24	-32	-42	-46	-50	-59	-67
40 mph	-13	-29	-45	-53	-60	-76	-92	64 kph	-25	-33	-43	-47	-51	-60	-69

through evaporation, you must wear clothes that breathe. Insulating your body from cold surfaces helps guard against heat loss through conduction. You can prevent heat loss through radiation by wearing layers of clothing and protecting your skin. Limiting your exposure to wind reduces heat loss through convection.

Wind Chill effects on humans

warmer than -19°C (-3°F)	Little additional effects with normal precautions.
-20°C to -36°C (-4°F to -33°F)	Thermal outer clothing required. Conditions unpleasant.
-36°C to –49°C (-34°F to -56°F)	Skin exposed to open air for a prolonged period of time begins to freeze.
-49°C to-58°C (-57°F to -72°F)	Exposed skin freezes within one minute. Outdoor travel is dangerous.
-58°C (-73°F) and colder	Exposed skin freezes within 30 seconds. Conditions are extremely dangerous.

It is important to keep warm, but without overheating yourself. Sweating cools the body by conducting heat away from the body. Sweat-damp clothing will not insulate you against the cold adequately. Wearing several layers of clothing is the key to warmth and survival. The outer layers of your clothing should provide ventilation while the inner layers provide insulation. Remember that several lightweight layers allow insulation space and will keep you warm more effectively.

Layers

For the innermost layer against your skin, use long underwear and a thermal undershirt. Wool or synthetic material that absorbs perspiration and draws it away from the skin works well as a substitute for a thermal undershirt. The second layer should be a loose-fitting, long-sleeved shirt that covers the wrists and neck. For the third layer, wear a light, fleecy jacket or woollen pullover. This third layer can readily be removed to prevent overheating. A hooded windproof or wind resistant jacket is necessary as the outermost garment to protect you from the wind. Features that allow you to vent the jacket in order to avoid overheating are a must. Mountain bibs may be worn over trousers

Layering against the cold

Keeping warm and dry is key in the cold. Protect yourself against extreme cold by covering exposed skin and layering clothing properly. Inner layers should draw mosture away from skin. Outer layers should be windproof and water resistant. To avoid overheating, outer layers should be vented or easily removed.

or alone as an outer layer. However, while these bibs do protect your legs from rain, they may cause overheating. They are best worn in subzero environments over lighter weight winter leggings.

Gloves

In order for you to be able to function in the cold it is essential that your hands remain warm. The layering principle applies to gloves as well. In the coldest situations the innermost layer should be silk glove liners, with woollen middle mittens and heavy, waterproof, insulated outer mittens. Two layers of gloves, with woollen finger gloves as the inner layer and insulated, waterproof mittens as the outer layer, will serve in situations that are not dangerously cold. In subzero temperatures, losing a glove can be deadly. Ensure that your outer mittens are attached to your jacket by a cord to alleviate the risk of dropping or misplacing them. An extra pair of socks can serve in an emergency as outer mittens, but only on a temporary basis. Socks are not designed to provide the level of protection for the hands that gloves are.

Boots

The best winter boots are calf-length and watertight. Purchase them in a size that will allow you to comfortably wear two pairs of socks underneath. If you do not own watertight boots, use snow gaiters to protect your feet from moisture. The layering of socks is important for warmth. The inner pair of socks can be thinner, but the outer layer of socks should be woollen and calf-length. It is important that your boots fit properly and are not too tight. Numbness in the feet can signal that the boots are too tight and are restricting circulation. Poor circulation makes you an ideal candidate for frostbite. Wiggle your toes every few minutes to ensure the circulation to your feet is not being cut off.

Head Protection

A significant amount of body heat is lost through the head. It is essential that your head and neck have adequate cover to maintain warmth. An insulated hat with ear flaps works well in combination with a warm scarf. In subzero temperatures it is better to wear a balaclava that protects the neck, the sides of the face and the head. The hood from your outermost jacket should then be worn over the balaclava. When in danger of overheating, the quickest way to vent excessive heat is to remove your head protection and loosen your scarf or any garments around your neck.

Clothing Care

Your clothing must be kept dry, clean and in good repair for it to properly insulate you from the cold. Before coming in from the cold, brush off any snow, slush or ice that has collected on your clothing. Repair any tears and wash any dirty clothing to maintain its maximum effectiveness in insulating you from the cold. The innermost layer of clothing will need frequent washing to remove the ingrained sweat and soil that can interfere with its ability to insulate.

FIRE BUILDING

Because warmth is a fundamental need if you are to survive extreme cold outdoors, building a fire is sometimes a necessity. Whether you are exposed to extreme cold in the outdoors by choice or accident, a small fire can both improve your morale and save your life.

Since winds that often accompany the cold can quench a fire, you must construct a protective barrier before you build and light a fire. A pit fire works best in calmer conditions, but an enclosed fire may be necessary in windier conditions.

Pit fires

A pit fire is built in a bowl-shaped depression. It is most effective to dig to a depth of about 30cm (1ft). This protects the fire from currents and breezes that can cause the fuel to burn too quickly.

Enclosed fires

An enclosed fire begins with the construction of a rock break about 60cm (2ft) high. Not only will the rocks trap the fire's heat, but they will also prevent the wind from scattering the embers.

Basic fire building

To build a fire, lay a base of green sticks side by side. Construct a pyramid of sticks by balancing four sticks against each other, selecting sticks that are larger than your finger in circumference. Their top ends should meet in a point. Continue to build up the pyramid of sticks, making sure it is sturdy and that you've left enough space at the bottom to insert the tinder that will get the fire going. Moss, bark, dead leaves, dry grass and small pieces of paper can serve as tinder. Place your tinder in the base of the pyramid and light it. You may add more leaves and twigs to encourage the flames. As the fire catches and grows, the pyramid will collapse inwards, feeding the heart of the fire and eventually producing a bed of hot embers.

Pit fire

When winds are relatively calm, a pit fire can be built for warmth. Useful for cooking, the pit prevents the wind from flaring the flames too severely. Because the flames in a pit fire are easier to control, it is also a good way to conserve fuel.

Enclosed fire

In windier conditions, construction of a rock wind break may be necessary to protect your fire and conserve fuel. Use only dry, non-porous rocks to build your break, avoiding sandstone or slate. Damp or porous rocks may explode when heated.

WATER

Water is your most urgent need in all climates. When surrounded by ice and snow, it is easy to forget that you may easily become dehydrated. Fortunately it is less of a challenge to acquire drinking water when surrounded by snow than in other environments.

No matter how thirsty you are do not eat snow, as eating snow lowers the body's temperature. By the same token, do not attempt to melt ice or snow in your mouth. Doing so can also lower your body temperature. Snow and freshwater ice can easily be melted for drinking water. Ice takes less time to melt than snow and yields more water than an equivalent amount of snow.

Place ice or snow in a container, such as a can or water bag, near the fire. Once that melts, slowly add more ice or snow and continue the melting process.

Inuit snow melter

An ingenious method for melting snow borrowed from the Inuit involves building a snow melter. Select two rocks, one smaller than the other, to provide the base.

Inuit snow melter

The Inuit snow melter works for melting either snow or ice. Build a small fire beneath a tilted stone slab. Arrange a series of small rocks in a V-shape to hold the snow or ice in place and direct the flow of water towards the receptacle at the slab's base.

Build a small fire between the rocks and place a slab of flat stone on the rock base. The slab of stone should rest at an angle to allow melted snow to run off. A v-shaped arrangement of small rocks will hold the snow in place and direct the water down the slab of stone towards a can or bucket. As the fire below heats the stone, the snow melts and runs off into the receptacle you've placed at the lower end of the stone slab.

If a fire is not available, a slower method for melting snow involves putting the ice or snow in a bag and placing the bag between layers of your clothing.

COLD INJURIES
Hypothermia

Hypothermia occurs when a person's body temperature drops to less than 35°C (95°F) and body heat is lost faster than it can be replaced. If body temperature drops to below 25°C (77°F), it is almost always lethal. This condition is possible even when temperatures are above freezing. For those who survive hypothermia, the legacy is often lasting physical ailments, including kidney, liver and pancreas problems. Symptoms of hypothermia are uncontrollable shivering, incoherence, memory loss, reduced coordination, disorientation, slurred speech, drowsiness and exhaustion.

Seek medical attention for hypothermia victims immediately. In the meantime, get the victim to a warm place. The victim must be warmed up again to restore the body's core temperature to normal. Remove the victim's clothing if it is wet. Cold, wet clothing accelerates heat loss. It is best to rewarm the hypothermia victim's torso first. Use warm water between the temperatures of 38° and 43°C (100° and 110°F). Attempting to rewarm the entire body at once in warm water is dangerous without a doctor's supervision. Improperly rewarming the body can drive cold blood from the hands and feet towards the heart, increasing the likelihood of shock and heart failure. If the person has not lost consciousness, have him sip hot, sweetened fluids. Do not force an unconscious person to drink.

Frostbite

Frostbite is a result of body tissues freezing. A wind chill of -29°C (-20°F) can cause frostbite to exposed skin in 30 minutes. The feet, hands, earlobes and exposed face are especially prone to frostbite. Superficial frostbite extends only to the skin. Deep frostbite extends to tissue beneath the skin, rendering those tissues stiff and solid. Advanced frostbite can lead to gangrene and the necessity to amputate the affected part.

Loss of feeling in the feet or hands is the first symptom of frostbite. Superficial frostbite appears as grey or yellowish patches on the skin. Deep frostbite appears as pale, waxy skin that feels cold and solid. When rewarmed, areas affected by deep frostbite may turn blue or purple and blister.

Seek medical attention immediately in cases of severe frostbite. Try to get the frostbite victim to a warm place as soon as possible. If symptoms indicate the frostbite is superficial, rewarm the affected area using water no hotter than 41°C (106°F) for 20 to 40 minutes. Skin-to-skin contact, such as holding a frostbitten hand between two warm hands or placing a frostbitten hand on a warm thigh also provides a safe method of slowly rewarming. Do not try to thaw severe frostbite. The injury can refreeze, causing more damage than the original frostbite injury.

In case of frostbite:

- Do not rub the affected area with snow or ice.
- Do not break any blisters that may have formed.
- Do not apply direct heat, such as fire or hot stones, to warm the affected area.
- Do not give the victim alcohol to drink. This will lower their body temperature.
- Do not rub the frostbitten area with your hands. This could result in tissue damage.

Immersion foot

Prolonged exposure to dampness can result in immersion foot. This condition is possible even in temperatures above freezing. Symptoms include cold, swollen, numb feet with a waxy appearance. Gangrene can develop if it is not treated, and in advanced cases the flesh dies and amputation is required.

Keeping the feet dry is the best prevention. Change into clean, dry socks daily. To treat symptoms, dry the feet and wiggle the toes to stimulate circulation. Elevate the legs to relieve pain and swelling, and allow them to warm naturally.

Dehydration and sunburn

These health hazards are particularly insidious because they are not typically anticipated in a cold environment. Body fluid lost through perspiration and absorbed into the heavy clothing must be replaced – your body requires water in the cold just as much as it does in a hot environment. Check the colour of your urine in the snow if you suspect you are becoming dehydrated. Dark yellow urine indicates you are dehydrating and need to replace lost fluids. Light yellow

Improvised sunglasses

Snow blindness is dangerous and painful. A good pair of sunglasses guards against damage from the sun's ultraviolet rays. If your sun glasses are lost or broken, you can improvise eye protection with a strip of dark negative film from your 35mm camera.

Improvised sunglasses

To protect against snow blindness, cut slits in a piece of cardboard, tree bark, or other material at hand. Use string or thread to secure your improvised sunglasses. Smearing soot beneath your eyes can also help cut down on reflected glare.

urine indicates that your body fluids are normally balanced.

Even though the temperature is below freezing, your skin is still susceptible to sunburn. White snow is a highly effective reflector of the sun's rays. Apply sun block to protect exposed skin from sun damage, and wear sunglasses or goggles to protect your eyes.

CROSSING ICE

Should the need arise to walk across a frozen body of water, proceed with extreme cau-

tion. Ice that is less than 8cm (3in) thick should be avoided. When walking across ice, always carry a long walking stick or a pair of ice awls, which are two pieces of wood with steel tips that can be stored in a jacket pocket. Both can help you free yourself if the ice breaks and you plunge into freezing water.

If you begin to feel the ice bending beneath you, get down on your stomach. This distributes your weight more evenly. Once on your stomach, wriggle your way back to shore.

FALLING THROUGH ICE

If the ice breaks and you find yourself submerged, try not to swallow any water. It will only serve to lower your core temperature. Swim back up to the hole you fell through and lay your walking stick flat across the ice to give yourself a solid object with which you can pull yourself out. If you have ice awls, you can use them to extricate yourself. Simply kick your legs to level off your body in the water as you dig into the surface ice with the ice awls. Once you have a good purchase on the ice with the ice awls, use them to pull yourself out of the water, then roll towards more solid ice.

To rescue someone you have witnessed falling through the ice, toss them a rope or extend a strong branch they can grab. Do not venture too close to the hole or jump in after them. If several people are available to assist, form a human chain by lying on your stomachs and holding hands to pull the person from the area of weakened ice. By lying down like this, everyone's weight will be more evenly distributed over the ice. It is also convenient in case the ice breaks beneath the rescuer closest to the original victim and you are suddenly faced with two people to fish out of the icy water.

Rolling in snow immediately after being plunged into icy water does absorb some of the excess moisture, but it is not a complete solution. It is essential that you immediately remove all wet clothing and warm up to guard against hypothermia. If you do not warm up, it will take approximately 20 minutes for your body to succumb to the cold and die. Rest for several hours. It will take that long for your body to recover.

WATCHES AND WARNINGS

As if freezing temperatures alone weren't perilous enough, winter can also bring storms that create flooding which threatens lives and property. Be certain you are familiar with the terms forecasters use to apprise the public of dangerous winter conditions.

Winter Weather Advisory: winter weather conditions are expected to cause significant inconveniences and may be hazardous, especially to motorists.

Frost/Freeze Warning: below-freezing temperatures are expected and may cause damage to plants, crops or fruit trees.

Winter Storm Watch: be alert, a storm is likely.

Winter Storm Warning: take action, the storm is in or entering the area

Flash Flood Watch or Flood Watch: be alert to signs of flash flooding and be ready to evacuate at short notice.

Flash Flood Warning: a flash flood is

imminent; act quickly to save yourself.

Flood Warning: flooding has been reported or is imminent; take necessary precautions at once.

Survivor's story

In 1992, Sir Ranulph Fiennes set out to cross the Antarctic with Dr Mike Stroud. Fiennes describes the excruciating pain associated with frostbite and how he dealt with it physically and psychologically.

'In the night I woke to stabbing pains from one frostbitten toe. Mike was asleep so I tried to emulate his scalpel incisions with my penknife. That seemed the best way of relieving the pressure. A good deal of pus and tea-like liquid escaped but the pains continued, so I swallowed two painkillers and eventually slept. I woke a few minutes later, or so it seemed, with a head full of rats. Mike checked the infected foot after porridge and squeezed it successfully.

"This is only local pus," he assured me.

'I cut out square-inch patches from my bed mat and plastered them all around the wound. This certainly helped the first few hours of travel by about three on a pain-scale of ten.

'My problem was the ongoing tunnel of pain, which made me irritable. If only it would go away at least some of the time. I found the sharp feel of it trying to wear me down.

'I realized how lucky I had been for fifty years of experiencing comparatively little pain. Broken bones and teeth, torn-off digits, frostbite and chronic kidney stones had seemed unpleasant at the time. But now I knew real pain and I feared lest it overwhelm me, to my everlasting shame.

'I tried to think up ways of attacking it mentally on the basis that, whenever there were lethal crevasses about or when navigational worries were preoccupying my brain, the constant pain receded. The pain

Falling through ice

Crossing ice is best avoided at all times. If you have to cross ice, carry some ice awls, which can be as simple as two pieces of wood with steel tips, in your pocket. If the ice breaks beneath you, use the awls to help haul yourself out of the icy water.

behaved like a circular railway track with a steam engine chugging relentlessly around it ... when it went through the tunnels it was still there but less noticeable. So I tried to invent tunnels, by day and by night, to program my mind with vivid thoughts of past happenings. When this failed, especially after I slipped or caught my boot and triggered raw shrieks from one or the other foot, I tried to imagine the pain as a living thing. Sometimes as a red-hot poker or an electric drill. At those times I would try to imagine I was part of the poker or the drill and I was working to stoke a fire or drill a gatepost. This would lead me to think of a myriad other 'jobs' that my pain could attack. I never won the fight with these tactics, but neither did I lose it.'

WINTERIZING YOUR VEHICLE

Extreme cold can be as difficult on a vehicle as it is on the human body. The key to protecting your vehicle from the cold lies in a few simple precautions. By winterizing your vehicle, you reduce the chances that the engine will stall, possibly leaving you stranded far away from assistance. These are a few simple steps you can take and supplies you can store in your vehicle before you venture out on a drive in subfreezing temperatures.

Check the tyres (tires)

- Check the tyre (tire) pressure. Colder temperatures actually lower pressure. Correct pressure is essential for proper traction. Add more air if your pressure falls below what is recommended by your owner's manual.
- Ensure that your tyres (tires) have good tread. Bald tyres (tires) will not allow proper breaking, especially on icy roads.
- If you regularly drive through snow, especially in hilly areas, purchasing a set of snow tyres (tires) is a good idea. Snow tyres (tires) are designed to improve traction on snowy roads and perform better under winter conditions than all-season tyres (tires).

Check the battery

- Be sure that battery terminals and cables are free of corrosion and firmly secured.
- Ask your mechanic to test the battery if it is more than three years old. Extreme cold can reduce a battery's power by up to 50 per cent.
- Distilled water should be added if the level does not cover the lead plates in your vehicle's battery.

Check the antifreeze

- In normal circumstances the proper mixture of water and antifreeze is 50 per cent water and 50 per cent antifreeze. This protects your radiator to temperatures reaching -29°C (-20°F).
- If you are in an area where temperatures are regularly lower than -29°C (-20°F), you will need to drain a small amount of the 50/50 mix from the radiator and replace the amount drained with straight antifreeze. If you do alter the mix of water and antifreeze in this way, remember that too much antifreeze can cause cooling problems in hot weather. Plan to drain the radiator and replace the antifreeze with a 50/50 mix when spring arrives.
- Auto parts suppliers carry inexpensive antifreeze testers that allow you to test the composition of your water and antifreeze mixture. If the ratio of the mixture is incorrect for the weather conditions, you can correct it by simply adding either antifreeze or water as needed.

Check the oil

- Make sure you change your oil at regular intervals. Dirty oil does not lubricate the engine as efficiently as clean oil does.
- Check your owner's manual to determine which type of oil your vehicle requires in

freezing weather. A thinner oil of a lower viscosity is appropriate for colder temperatures because it circulates better.

Check the windscreen (windshield) wipers and fluid

- If your wiper blades are more than six months old, replace them. Visibility is key for safe driving in winter conditions and old wiper blades will not clear the windscreen (windshield) effectively.
- Use a wiper fluid that will not freeze. Make sure the reservoir is replenished at regular intervals. Travel on slushy streets and gritty or salted roads will mean that you will need to use your wipers to clean your windscreen (windshield) frequently.
- Before starting your car and turning on your wipers, ensure that they have not frozen to the windscreen (windshield) while sitting in the cold. If you turn them on when they are frozen to the windscreen (windshield), you could damage the wiper blade, the wiper fuse or the wiper motor.

Check the belts and hoses

- Ask a mechanic to check the condition of your belts and hoses before winter begins and replace any that are worn. Extremely cold temperatures are hard on them.

Check the four-wheel-drive system

- Before winter, make sure the four-wheel-drive system engages and disengages smoothly, and that the drivetrain is not noisy when the system is in use.
- Check the transmission and gear oil levels and add more of these fluids if levels are low.
- Be sure that all drivers of the vehicle know how to use the four-wheel-drive system properly.
- Check your owner's manual to find out at what speeds and in what conditions the four-wheel-drive can be activated.

Human chain for ice rescue

In the absence of a rope or branch to hold out to a person who has fallen through ice, form a human chain to pull the person out. One person should kneel on dry land and hold fast to

Protect your paint

- Start winter with a coat of wax. The ice, snow, salt and grit of winter can damage your vehicle's finish.
- Wash your vehicle often during winter, remembering to clean the wheel wells

the legs of a second person, who can lie across the ice to where the victim is . Lying flat distributes your weight more evenly and decreases the chances of the ice breaking beneath you before as you perform the rescue.

and under the body of the vehicle where slush, salt and grit are splashed.

Carry an emergency kit
- Torch (flashlight)
- Flares
- First aid kit and manual
- An ice scraper and snow brush
- Snow shovel
- Extra washer fluid
- Tool kit
- Jumper cables

Survival kit for your car

A first aid kit and manual, blanket, ice scraper, torch (flashlight), tow chain, jumper cables, knife, tool kit, duct tape, and emergency flare are a few of the essential items you'll need in case you become stranded in your car.

- Distress flag
- Duct tape or electrical·tape
- Toilet paper
- Knife
- Tow chain
- A bag of abrasive material which will allow you to gain traction when a tyre (tire) is stuck. Sand, snow-melt, salt, or non-clumping cat litter work well.
- An extra change of warm clothing
- Boots
- Blanket
- Water and non-perishable food
- Change for a pay phone or a calling card

DRIVING IN THE COLD

The leading cause of fatalities during the winter season is transportation accidents. Once you prepare your vehicle for surviving the cold, there are guidelines to follow to ensure your safety while driving.

- Always wear your seat belt.
- Slow down and triple the distance between you and the vehicle ahead of you.
- Change lanes and proceed through intersections with great caution.
- Drive with your headlamps (headlights) on. This makes it easier for other vehicles to see you.
- Keep windows, mirrors and lights free of ice or snow.
- If your vehicle has anti-lock brakes, press the brake pedal and hold it there. Do not pump the brakes.
- If you do not have anti-lock brakes and your brakes lock, remove your foot from the brake pedal for a moment.
- If you begin to skid on a slick surface, steer into the skid. For example, if the back end of your vehicle begins skidding to the right, turn the steering wheel to the right.
- Accelerate gently to avoid spinning the tyres (tires).
- If you must drive during a winter weather advisory or winter storm watch, travel during daylight, do not travel alone, stay on the main roads and be sure someone knows what route you are taking.
- When at all possible, avoid driving during a winter storm warning.
- Keep your fuel tank full. This will prevent ice from forming in the fuel tank or fuel lines.
- Monitor your radio for the most recent reports on road conditions.

Stranded in a vehicle

You may easily become trapped far from help if your vehicle stalls or becomes stuck in an extremely cold environment. Should this happen in a remote area, it is important that you stay warm and make your vehicle visible to rescuers.

- Turn on hazard flashers (warning lights).
- Remain in the vehicle to stay warm.
- Run the motor and heater for approximately ten minutes each hour to stay warm. Do not run it continuously as this will waste valuable fuel.
- Turn on the vehicle's interior light at night while running the engine to increase your visibility to rescuers.
- Hang a distress flag or brightly coloured cloth from your radio antenna or door.
- Check that the exhaust pipe is not blocked. Dangerous fumes can back up into your vehicle if it is blocked.
- Open a window a little bit to allow in fresh air and prevent carbon monoxide poisoning. If possible, open the window on the side of the vehicle away from blowing wind.
- Keep your blood circulating by periodically moving your arms, legs, fingers and toes vigorously. This will help keep you warm. Do not overexert yourself.
- Try not to stay in one position for too long.
- Huddle up with other passengers.
- Wrap yourself in a blanket. If you have not included a blanket in your vehicle's emergency kit, you can improvise by covering up with road maps, newspapers, extra clothing, seat covers or floor mats. Anything that will provide extra insulation is helpful.
- If it is not storming and you recall seeing a building where you could obtain assistance or shelter, bundle up and walk along the road to get there. Following the road allows passing motorists or rescuers to spot you. It is easy to become disoriented while walking across open country.

First aid kit contents

A well-stocked first aid kit is an essential item for every household. The most important things that it should include adhesive bandages, gauze pads, tape, cotton wool, swabs, scissors, tweezers, antiseptic, iodine, a thermometer, latex gloves, a small sewing kit, sun block, and prescription medications. Check your first aid kit monthly, replacing items and disposing of any out-of-date medication as necessary.

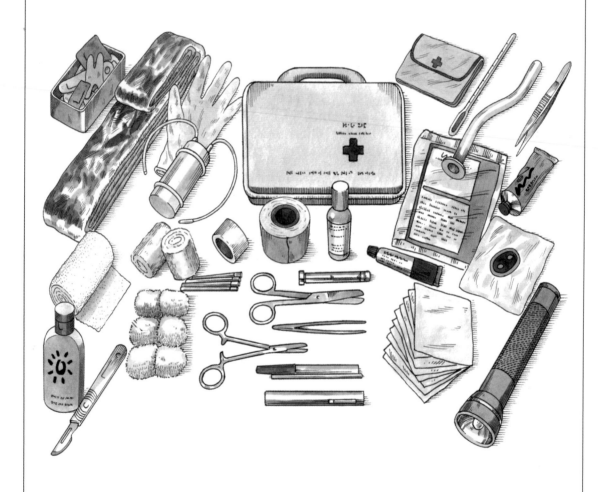

WINTERIZNG YOUR HOME

In order to keep warm and reduce heating costs, it is important to prepare your home from the cold before winter arrives. Methods for protecting your home from the cold are discussed earlier. The following list offers additional steps you can take to prevent damage from freezing and minimize heat loss from the home. These measures are particularly helpful in areas where cold snaps, rather than sustained periods of freezing weather, occur.

- Install outside tap (faucet) covers. This will protect your outside spigots from freezing.
- Wrap exposed pipes outdoors with newspapers and plastic.
- Drape shrubbery and other plants with a layer of cloth, then a layer of plastic on top of that to prevent them from freezing.
- Close the shades or drapes at night. This will cut down on unwanted air currents.
- Close off all unused rooms. It is more energy efficient to heat only those rooms that are in use.
- The draught-blocking rubber strip across the bottom of your doors should be replaced if it looks damaged or worn.
- Keep space heaters at least one metre (3ft) from any flammable objects.
- If using kerosene heaters, refuel them outside and maintain ventilation while in use to prevent the build-up of toxic fumes.

Pets

Remember that pets and livestock are sus-ceptible to some of the same cold injuries as humans. Animals can suffer and die if left out in the cold. Ensure that all of your animals have warm shelter and ample food and water.

BASIC PREVENTION

When exposed to extreme cold, use the buddy system to keep an eye on each other for signs of frostbite or hypothermia. Dress properly using layers to insulate and stay as dry as conditions allow. Even if you are in a shelter, you may want to wrap yourself in a thermal or foil emergency blanket, covering your neck and heat to protect against heat loss.

While some amount of movement promotes circulation and helps keep you warm, bear in mind that it also burns calories and increases your need for water. The strain from vigorous activity in the cold, such as pushing a stuck vehicle, can result in a heart attack. Do not overexert yourself.

When stranded, extreme cold and the effects of dehydration can make you feel lethargic. Apathy is deadly in freezing temperatures. It is important to remain clear thinking and remind yourself that the situation you are in is not a permanent one. You must not succumb to indifference. Mild exercise or even a conversation with a companion can dispel apathy. When faced with sub-zero weather, you must draw on your reserves of self-sufficiency. Monitor your physical and psychological condition constantly and, above all, remain calm and alert.

CHAPTER SEVEN

Extreme Heat

The human body cannot function longer than three days in a hot climate without water. A 5% body fluid loss results in thirst and weakness. A 10% loss means headaches and difficulty walking. If 15% or more is lost the result is death. Knowing how to dress in the heat, construct shelter, and acquire water can save your life.

Whether at home or in the desert, exposure to extreme heat is a hazard. Extreme heat is defined as temperatures that reach 10 degrees or higher above the average high temperature for the area and persist for several weeks. High-pressure systems can trap hazy, damp air near the ground, adding to the misery by making conditions humid. Dry, hot conditions can give rise to dust storms and, if they last long enough, create a drought. Deserts are automatically associated with extreme heat, but urban areas are also at risk. The build-up of heat-absorbing pollutants combined with the urban building blocks of brick, asphalt and concrete, which easily absorb heat and re-radiate it for long periods, make cities hotter than surrounding rural areas. A prolonged heat wave in an already hot city can produce sustained temperatures that are just as dangerous as temperatures in a sandy desert at noon.

HEAT AND THE HUMAN BODY

Heat incapacitates and kills by rapidly depleting the water in your body and driving your body temperature to dangerous heights. There are more than three million sweat glands in your skin producing perspiration, which cools the body. An increase in body temperature, whether from exertion or a high air temperature, causes you to sweat more. The more sweating you do, the more fluids your body loses. High humidity complicates an already unpleasant situation by increasing dehydration and preventing heat loss when sweat evaporates.

The sun pounding down on you is not the only way your body gains heat. The sun's rays reflected off of surfaces, hot winds and conducted heat from direct contact with heated objects all contribute to heat you.

If you find yourself in a desert survival situation, you'll face a variety of environmental challenges, including low rainfall, intense heat, sparse vegetation, extremely bright light levels, wide temperature fluctuations, sandstorms and mirages.

- Deserts by definition receive less than 25cm (10in) of rainfall annually. Some receive less than 10cm (4in) annually.
- Air temperatures may reach as high as 60°C (140°F). Sand and rocks get even hotter than the air.
- Temperatures at night can plummet to 10°C (50°F) and chill those without adequate clothing.
- Lack of vegetation increases the difficulty of finding water and ready shelter.
- Intense light levels can harm unprotected eyes to the point of causing temporary blindness.
- Sandstorms can pummel you with stinging sand propelled by winds with speeds of up to 129 kph (80 mph).
- Mirages are optical illusions caused by light refracted through rising, heated air. A mirage makes faraway objects appear to move and blurs them beyond identification.

SANDSTORM SURVIVAL

If caught in a sandstorm, take shelter immediately. Crouch behind a rock, facing away from the wind. Keep the blowing sand off your skin and out of your clothing as much as possible by covering your head, neck and shoulders with a jacket or any other piece of available material. If no object is available to act as a wind block, lie flat and cover your head, neck and shoulders. Wait until the sandstorm passes before attempting to move on.

HOT WEATHER CLOTHING

The clothing you wear in hot environments must help maintain your core body temperature. In the desert, clothes must do double duty by protecting against harsh heat and sunlight during the day and keeping you warm during the cold nights. As with cold-weather clothing, layering is important to provide insulation and ventilation.

Layers

At the innermost layer, wear a T-shirt made of cotton in a pale colour and underwear that will absorb sweat and draw it away from the skin. Wear a long-sleeved, lightweight cotton shirt over the T-shirt and roll the sleeves down to protect the arms from sunburn. Wear loose-fitting trousers of lightweight cotton that are sturdy enough to protect the legs from sunlight and blowing sand. To protect against sand-laden winds and the cold of the night wear a lightweight, windproof jacket as the outermost layer.

Protecting the head, feet and eyes

A wide-brimmed hat with eyelet vents in the brim keeps off the sun. Baseball hats and felt hats are a poor choice because they retain heat. For footwear, select lightweight boots with sturdy soles. All of your clothing should be light in colour to reflect sunlight. Darker coloured clothing absorbs heat. Sunglasses are absolutely necessary to protect the eyes from harmful ultra-violet rays and blowing sand.

Wearing a bandana or handkerchief loosely around the neck will absorb sweat and block the sun. If dampened and worn around the neck, it can aid in cooling the body.

SHELTER

Natives of desert regions usually travel at night when it is cooler. Rest under any available trees and avoid exertion, which could lead to fluid loss. If there are no trees available, improvise a shelter by draping a blanket or piece of material over a length of string. Tie the string between two rock piles or stakes to create a primitive pup tent. Scoop out a pit in the sand to lie in and place a protective layer between your body and the hot ground.

If you remain still in the shade, fully

Layering against the heat

Layers of clothing must protect the skin from sun exposure during the day and help retain body heat at night. Clothing should be made of strong, lightweight material. It should also be light-coloured to help reflect the sun's rays to keep you cooler.

Desert shelter

Dig a trench 46–61cm (18–24 in) deep that is long and wide enough to lie down in comfortably. Pile the sand dug from the trench around three sides, forming a mound. Cover the trench with material, such as a poncho or canvas tarp, anchoring the material by piling sand on it. If a second layer of material is available, create a second layer 30–46cm (12–18 in) above the first one.

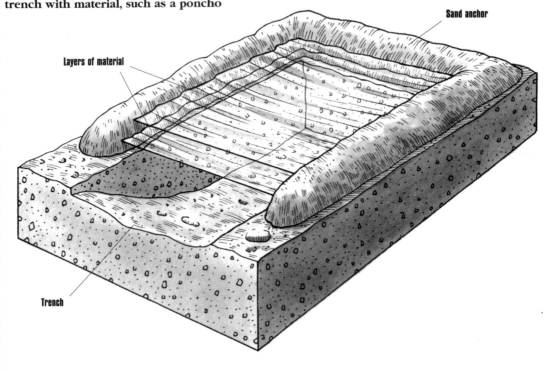

Sand anchor

Layers of material

Trench

clothed, breathing through your nose with your mouth closed, you reduce the amount of water you need to survive. Do not take off your shirt to cool down. Your cotton shirt will keep you cool by absorbing sweat and protecting you from sunburn.

WATER

The body loses fluids naturally through sweating, urinating and defecating. The average adult loses and must replace 2–3 litres (4–6 pints) of water each day. This figure is doubled when you are exerting yourself and tripled in very hot regions.

Procuring water is your most pressing priority in a hot climate. The human body can only survive for about three days without water. If you do nothing but rest in the shade, you can live, albeit miserably, for anywhere from 5 to 12 days without water, depending on the temperature.

You cannot accurately judge how much water you need based on thirst alone. As a rule of thumb, drink 500ml (one pint) of water every hour when temperatures are below 38°C (100°F), and drink one litre (one quart) of water every hour when temperatures are above 38°C (100°F). Drink water before you are thirsty. Rationing your water supply is a bad idea and can result in heat casualties, so drink plenty. Procure and purify more water when you begin to run low.

If water is scarce you should not eat. The digestion process requires water. Eating will use up valuable body fluids your body needs to use to cool itself.

There are many stories about people who drank their own blood or urine to survive. When faced with the alternatives of consuming your own body fluids or nothing at all, opt for nothing at all. Urine will only

dehydrate you further as it contains harmful body wastes and is about two per cent salt. Blood is much saltier than urine and requires as much energy and body fluids to digest as food. Since you can survive without food for about three weeks, you can afford to put off drinking your own blood for just as long.

Finding water

If there are no surface bodies of water available, there will be clues to help you locate hidden water. Trees and other vegetation require water. Bees and flies never travel far

Finding water

In the absence of green vegetation, which is the best sign of the presence of water, a seemingly dry riverbed can yield water. Dig where the riverbed makes a sharp turn on the outside bank or where it encounters a rock barrier.

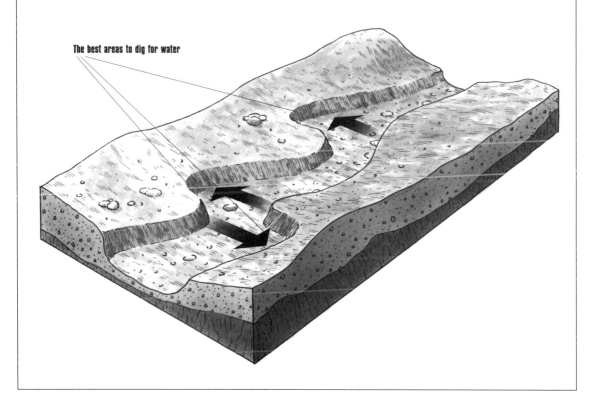

The best areas to dig for water

Water requirements for desert survival

At Rest in the Shade

°F	°C	No water at all	3 litres (3 quarts)	8 litres (8 quarts)
122	50	2-5 days	2-5 days	3-5 days
86	30	7 days	5-8 days	14 days
68	20	12 days	14 days	23-25 days

Walking at Night

122	50	1 day	2 days	3-5 days
86	30	4 days	5 days	5-7 days
68	20	9 days	10-15 days	5-15 days

(Source: McManners, Hugh. The Complete Wilderness Training Book. New York: Dorling Kindersley Publishing, Inc., 1994.)

from water sources. Converging animal tracks can lead you to a water source.

When digging for water, choose a spot in a low-lying area, at the foot of concave banks of dry riverbeds, at the foot of cliffs or rock outcroppings or where there is damp surface sand. Dig a hole deep enough to allow water to seep in.

If barrel cactus grows in the area, it can be a source of water. Slice off the top of the cactus and mash the pulp. Suck the juice out of the pulp, then discard it. Do not eat the pulp. Be careful not to try this with the giant saguaro cactus that grows in the American Southwest. The saguaro's fluids are poisonous.

Water purification

Once you procure water, you must filter and purify it before you drink it. By drinking water that has not been purified you can contract dysentery, cholera or typhoid. The diarrhoea accompanying these ailments will only serve to dehydrate you further.

Filtering

You can use a clean sock, cloth bag or trouser leg as a filtering device. Remember that filtering only clears the water. To make it safe for drinking, you must also purify the water.

Tripod filter

Create a tripod by lashing three long sticks together at one end with twine. Assuming you are using a sock, line the sock with a layer of sand or a handkerchief. Suspend the sock from the tripod over a can or other collection device. Pour water into the sock and allow it to drip slowly into the can. Rinse out the sock after each filtering pass.

Cloth bag filter

Use a cloth bag or trouser leg. Tie one end shut and fill it with several layers of filtering material, such as sand, crushed rock or cloth. Suspend it over a can, pour water into the top and allow the filtered water to drip out.

Purifying

The simplest method of purifying water is to boil it vigorously for at least 10 minutes. The higher your altitude, the longer boiling time water requires. Add an extra minute of boiling time for each 300m (1000ft) you are above sea level.

If you prefer the chemical purification route, iodine, chlorine and potassium permanganate are the most popular purifiers.

Iodine: Add 10 drops to one litre (one quart) of clear water or 20 drops to cloudy water. Iodine gives the water a pink tinge and has a distinctive taste.

Chlorine Bleach: Add eight drops to 4.5 litres (one gallon) of clear water or sixteen drops to cloudy water. Be sure the active

Water filtration

To filter water, place several layers of filtering material in a cloth bag or trouser leg. Tie one end shut. Crushed rock, sand, or cloth all make good filtering material. Suspend the filter over a receptacle, pour water into the top, and allow the water to work its way through the filtering materials.

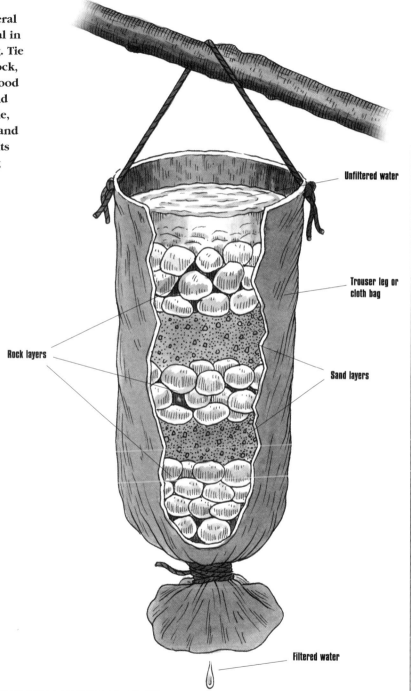

Unfiltered water

Trouser leg or cloth bag

Rock layers

Sand layers

Filtered water

Saltwater still

A saltwater still is an effective way to distill potable water. Boil the salty water in a can with a cloth placed over the top. The cloth will capture steam. Use a series of cloths to collect steam. Remove the hot cloths from the can with a stick. Wring the purified water out of the cloths once they've cooled enough to handle.

ingredient is sodium hypochlorite at 5.25 per cent in the bleach you use. If you have chlorine tablets, add one tablet per 500ml (one pint) of water.

Potassium Permanganate: Add enough to tinge the water a light pink colour.

Distilling salty water
To purify salty water, build a saltwater still. Construct a tripod and build a small fire beneath it. Suspend a can full of water from the tripod over the flame. Place a clean cloth over the top of the can. The cloth will collect steam as the water boils. Use a series of cloths, one at a time. To avoid burning your hands on the hot cloth, lift it off the can with a stick. When the cloths have cooled sufficiently, wring the purified water out of them into a container.

Underground solar water still
You can collect water from the soil by constructing an underground solar water still. The temperature difference between the sun and the soil will cause water to condense on your still.

- Choose an area where the soil is likely to harbour moisture and the sunlight strikes most of the day.
- Dig a bowl-shaped hole about 60cm (2ft) deep and 1m (3ft) wide.
- Place a container at the bottom of the hole.
- If you have a tube available, place one end in the container and run the other end out of the hole.
- Place a plastic sheet across the top of the hole and cover the edges with soil to hold it in place. Rocks can also be used to hold the edges of the plastic down.
- Put a fist-sized rock directly in the middle of the sheet, right over the container.
- Lower the rock about 40cm (15in) below ground level, keeping it suspended above

the container.
- Be sure the plastic that is suspended in the hole does not touch the sides of the hole.
- Add more soil or rocks round the edges of the plastic to hold it in place and prevent moisture from escaping.
- Plug the tube when not using it to drink from the container to prevent the moisture from evaporating.

As the sun heats the air in the hole, water vapour condenses on the underside of the plastic sheet and drips into the container. Dig another hole for a new still when the moisture from the original hole has been depleted.

Aboveground water still
This variety of still requires plants and a sunny slope.

- Fill a clear plastic bag 1/2 to 3/4 full of green vegetation
- Place a rock or some other weight in the bag.
- Tie the bag shut as securely as possible. Be sure to leave air in the bag.
- Place the bag on a sunny slope. The rock should rest at the lowest place in the bag.

Condensed water will collect round the rock. Do not use poisonous vegetation in this still. It will produce poisonous fluid.

HEAT INJURIES
Heat injuries occur when you have overexposed your body to heat or overexerted yourself. Heat injuries aren't restricted to hot climates; you can succumb to heat stress anywhere – from the desert to the city.

Heat cramps
Caused by loss of salt due to excess sweating, heat cramps are muscular pains and

Unerground solar water still

Choose a site that receives sunlight most of the day. Place a container in the bottom of the hole and run tubing from the container to the surface. Plastic sheeting across the top of the hole should be anchored with soil. Place a rock in the center of the plastic, directly over the container. Moisture will condense on the plastic and drip into the container.

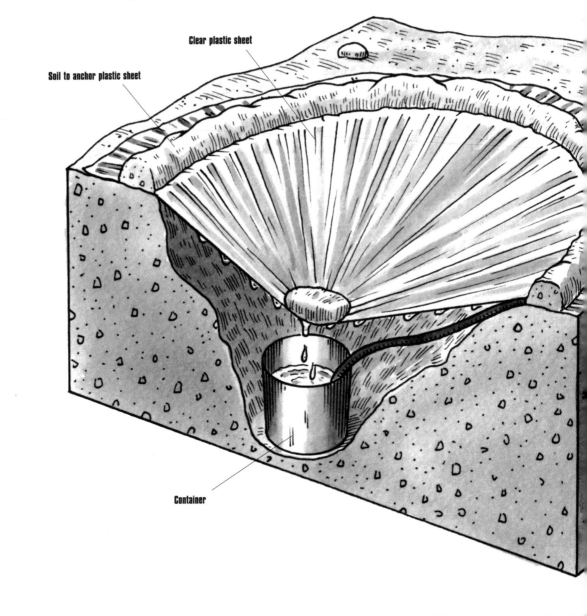

Clear plastic sheet

Soil to anchor plastic sheet

Container

Drinking tube

spasms. Heavy exertion can bring on this condition. Symptoms include moderate to severe muscle cramps in the legs, arms or abdomen. When these cramps begin, move the victim into the shade and administer small amounts of water to drink every three minutes. Untreated, this condition could escalate to heat exhaustion or heat stroke.

Heat exhaustion

Heat exhaustion is caused by a loss of salt and body fluids. Blood flow to the skin increases, decreasing blood flow to vital organs, and results in mild shock. Symptoms include headache, irritability, confusion, weakness, dizziness, sweating, cramps and pale, clammy skin. Get the victim out of the sun immediately. Remove any excess clothing and apply cool, wet cloths to the skin. If the victim has not lost consciousness, administer half a glass of cool water to drink every 15 minutes. Drinks containing alcohol or caffeine can aggravate the condition.

Heat stroke

Also referred to as sunstroke, this is a potentially fatal condition caused by extreme loss of water and salt. Seek medical attention immediately. The body ceases to cool itself, so there is an urgent need to cool the victim. Symptoms include hot, red skin; vomiting; loss of consciousness; rapid, weak pulse; rapid, shallow breathing; and body temperature as high as 40.5°C (105°F). Move the victim to a cooler place and immerse in cool water or wrap wet sheets around the body. Lie the victim down and turn a fan towards him. If he refuses water, do not force him to drink.

Sunburn

Overexposing your skin to the rays of the sun results in sunburn. Symptoms include skin redness and pain, blisters, fever and headache. You must wear protective clothing and liberally apply sun block to all exposed skin. Even on overcast days, sunburn is possible. Do not

Aboveground water still

A plastic bag containing green, leafy vegetation makes a simple still. Place the bag on a slope in full sunlight. A rock inside the bag will anchor it. Moisture will condense from the plants and gather at the low end of the bag around the rock.

forget to periodically re-apply sun block that has been washed away by perspiration.

Survivor's story

In 1986, Michael Asher set out to cross the Sahara desert on camel. He describes the physical and psychological effects the extreme heat had on him, his wife Marinetta and their guide Mafoudh.

'The next day we rode across a rolling plain of stubbled grass with the hot wind chasing us. It was the hottest day of the hottest season. The land seemed burning. The wind blew in flame-thrower blasts. It was hotter than Chinguetti in June, hotter than anything I had experienced in the eastern Sahara. Everything was glaring hot – the saddle, the stick in my hands and the folds of my shirt. My hands and feet were swollen from the roasting; my throat felt like emery paper; my gums were choked with a paste of mucus. The wind rose and fell in gusts. When it hit us it was like being braised with hot, dripping fat. When it fell the stillness of the air brought beads of sweat to our heads at once. I was glad of the protection of my thick head-cloth, swirling shirt and pantaloons, which allowed the circulation of cool air beneath, but nothing could ease my parched mouth or the nausea in my stomach.

'As midday approached we searched vainly for a tree. In the whole of that vast landscape there was none. Instead we had to put up our tent. The sand was too hot to stand on. Even in sandals you could feel the heat cutting through."If you broke an egg on this, it would fry" Marinetta said. Inside the tent it was stifling but just better than the inferno outside. Marinetta made zrig in two minutes. As Mafoudh drank, my eyes were riveted on the bowl. He seemed to drink and drink. I could see his Adam's apple working up and down as he swallowed. It seemed he would never pass it to me. When he did so, I thought, "He drank so

Sources of heat gain

The sun's direct rays are not the only source of heat. Hot, blowing winds and heat reflected off sand increase heat. The temperature of sand and rock is higher than air temperature. Direct contact with heated sand and rocks also raises temperature.

Direct rays from sun

Hot, blowing winds

Direct contact with heated rocks or sand

Reflected heat

much!" Then I tilted it to my lips, noticing Marinetta's suspicious, beady eyes tracking my every move. It was indescribably wonderful to feel the thick, sugary milk slip down my throat, easing the raw skin of the mouth and reinflating my shrunken stomach. I passed it to my wife. She almost snatched it from me and glared at me accusingly when she saw what was left.

'Our bodies were already streaming with sweat as the liquid re-hydrated our cells and was flushed out by the cooling mechanism of the sweat glands. For an instant there was an intensely pleasant sensation of coolness. But the feeling soon passed, to be replaced by the beginning of another nagging thirst. It was too hot to cook, so Mafoudh made

Effects of dehydration

5% body fluid loss

10% body fluid loss

15% body fluid loss

tea. Then we just lay there in wet heaps, praying to God to take the heat away. I couldn't believe that any conditions, not those of the Poles, nor of the jungles nor of the open sea, could be worse than the Sahara in summer.'

Terms to know

Heat Wave: This is a prolonged period of excessive heat and humidity.

Heat Index: This is a number in degrees

With 5 per cent body fluid loss comes thirst, weakness, irritability, and nausea. A 10 per cent loss results in headache, dizziness, and difficulty walking. When 15 per cent is lost, the effects are dim vision, deafness, swollen tongue, painful urination, and numbness. If more than 15% body fluid is lost, the result is death.

More than 15% body fluid loss

BASIC PREVENTION
At home

- Install temporary reflectors in the windows, such as aluminium foil, to reflect heat away from the home.
- Protect windows by hanging shades, drapes, shutters or awnings on windows that receive full afternoon or morning sun.
- Remain indoors as much as possible.
- Eat nutritional, light meals.
- Drink plenty of water.
- Limit your alcohol consumption. Alcohol accelerates dehydration.
- Wear a wide-brimmed hat outdoors.
- Wear lightweight, loose-fitting clothing.
- Stay out of the sun as much as possible and apply sun block regularly.
- Do not overexert yourself.
- Only take salt tablets if your physician directs you to do so.
- If drought conditions exist, limit your water usage by cutting back on car washing and lawn watering.

In the desert

- Tell someone where you are going and when you will return.
- If you are with others, watch one another for signs of heat exhaustion, heat stroke or sunburn.
- Drink water at least once an hour.
- Rest in the shade.
- Place a barrier between your body and the hot ground while resting.
- Check the colour of your urine for signs of dehydration. Light-coloured urine indicates your fluid levels are safe. Darker urine means you need to drink more fluids.

Desire to survive

Heat and thirst can conspire to make you irritable and impatient. Do not give up hope of being rescued or making your way through the ordeal. With a little ingenuity and perseverance, you can survive even the hottest desert.

Fahrenheit (°F) that tells how hot it really feels when the relative humidity is added to the actual air temperature. Exposure to full sunshine can increase the heat index by as much as 15°F.

CHAPTER EIGHT

Heavy Snowfall

Heavy snowfall brings the dangers of avalanches and snowblindness and hypothermia and and presents considerable barriers to mobility. Knowing how to drive in snow, build shelters, survive an avalanche and signal rescuers will enable you to master the snowiest environment.

To survive a heavy snowfall you must have warm clothing and a place to shelter. Snowfall can increase the difficulty of travel and render it more difficult to obtain your basic needs of water and shelter. Heavy accumulations of snow can collapse roofs, close airports, kill livestock and cause avalanches.

A blizzard is the most severe of winter storms. The blowing snow associated with blizzards can reduce visibility to just a few metres (yards). These conditions render it anywhere from hazardous to impossible to drive. People caught outdoors during blizzards can rapidly lose their way and freeze to death. People travelling without car survival kits have frozen to death in trapped cars while awaiting rescue. Power and telephone lines are often damaged during blizzards, leaving people trapped in their homes unable to get necessary food and supplies.

Blizzards are difficult to predict. The heaviest snowfalls usually occur when temperatures are around freezing. Meteorologists watch for Arctic air masses approaching from the north and gauge whether the air is cold enough in the lower atmosphere to generate snow. Three key components form winter storms. The first is the freezing air in the clouds and near the ground necessary for ice and snow to form. The second is moisture from water evaporating off of lakes or oceans. The third is lift, or the rising of an air mass, which forms clouds and precipitation.

Ice and snow injuries

- Approximately 70 per cent result from vehicle accidents.
- Approximately 25 per cent are sustained by people caught out in a winter storm.
- Most happen to males over the age of 40.

(Source: NOAA)

WINTER WEATHER TERMS

Blizzard: Winds of 56 kilometres (35 miles) per hour or greater with snow and blowing snow reducing visibility to less than 400m (1/4 mile) for at least three hours.

Blowing snow: Wind-driven snow that reduces visibility. It may be falling snow or snow lifted from the ground by winds.

Snow squalls: Brief but intense snow showers with strong, gusty winds. Accumulation may be significant.

Snow showers: Snow falling at varying intensities for brief periods of time. Some accumulation is possible.

Snow flurries: Light snow falling for a short duration with little or no accumulation.

WATCHES AND WARNINGS

Winter Weather Advisory: Winter weather conditions are expected to cause significant inconveniences and may prove hazardous, especially to motorists.

Winter Storm Watch: A winter storm is possible in your area.

Winter Storm Warning: A winter storm is occurring or will soon occur in your area.

Blizzard Warning: Combined snow and strong winds will produce blinding snow, visibility near zero, deep drifts and life-threatening wind chill. Take shelter immediately.

Frost or Freeze Warning: Temperatures below freezing are expected.

CLOTHING

You must have sufficient layers of winter clothing and keep vital areas of heat loss protected if you are to survive heavy snow. The

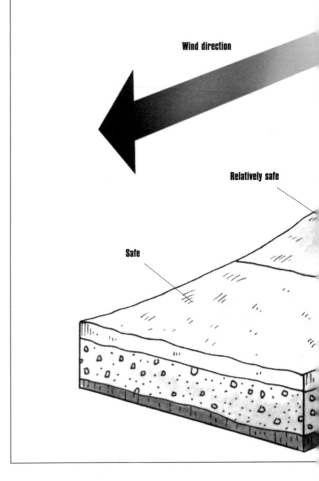

Danger zones for avalanche

Convex slopes hold the most avalanche risk. Steep south-facing slopes that have been sun-warmed through the day are dangerous because they are less stable. In the southern hemisphere this is true of north-facing slopes. Skiers, loud noises, or seismic activity can trigger an avalanche.

Wind direction

Relatively safe

Safe

head, neck, wrists and ankles radiate quite a bit of heat and must be insulated.

Clothing should be worn loose and in layers because tight clothing restricts circulation. Poor circulation leads to cold injuries.

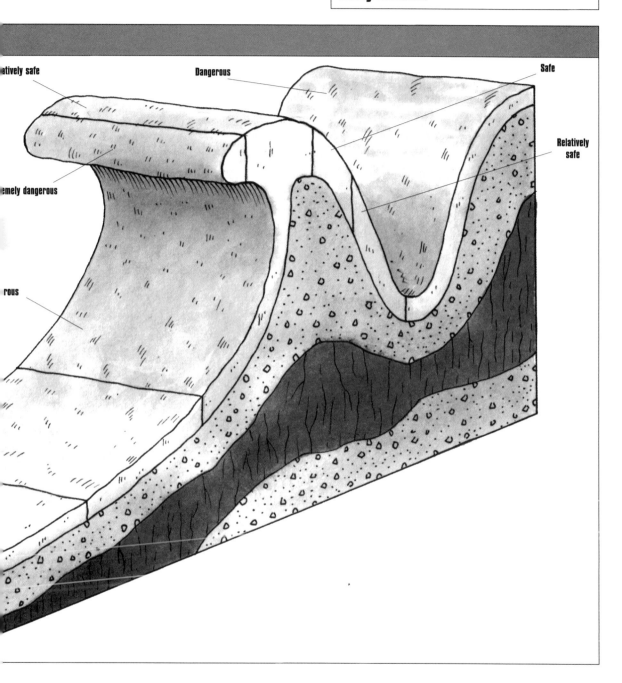

Relatively safe

Dangerous

Safe

Extremely dangerous

Relatively safe

Dangerous

Multiple layers allow for dead air space between the layers, which helps insulate against cold. Outer layers can be removed to prevent overheating and sweating. Complete details on layering are outlined earlier.

Clothing must be kept dry for it to adequately warm you. Inner layers may become wet from perspiration. Outer clothing should be water repellent. It is often impossible to keep clothing dry in blizzard conditions, so it

Igloo

Igloo construction is labour intensive. They are excellent shelters if you plan to remain in one place for a while. Cut out blocks from deep-packed snow. Arrange the bottom layer in a circle then trim the tops so they spiral upwards. Continue adding layers of blocks and top it off with a cap block.

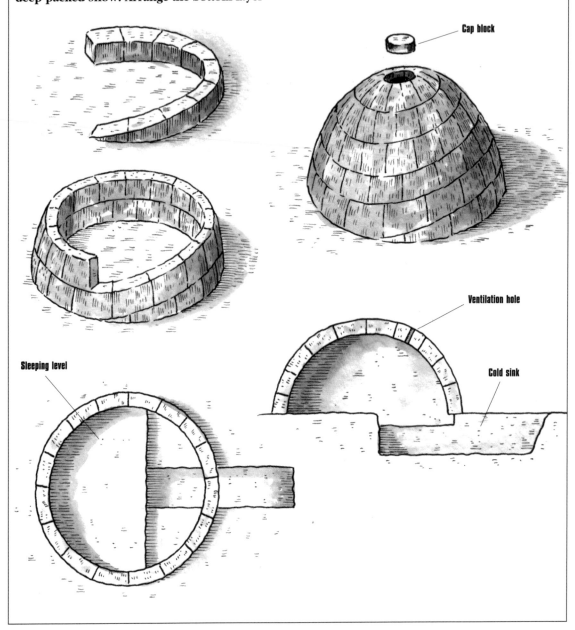

Cap block

Ventilation hole

Cold sink

Sleeping level

is important to brush off excess snow before entering a warm shelter. Damp socks or mittens can be dried by placing them between layers of your clothing where your body heat will dry them. Once in your shelter, you can dry clothing items by holding them near a source of heat. If the heat is too intense for your hands, it is too intense for your clothing. Move away from the fire until you can comfortably hold the clothing up by hand.

Clothing must be kept clean. This is important not only for hygiene, but also in terms of how effectively the clothing can warm you. Dirty garments do not insulate as effectively as clean ones.

Do not allow yourself to become overheated. The perspiration produced when you overheat soaks into your clothing and the sweat-soaked clothing will not insulate to its fullest capabilities. The evaporating sweat also acts to cool your body. Remove a layer of clothing to avoid overheating. A quick way to vent excess body heat is to temporarily remove your head cover and loosen your scarf or the neck of your jacket.

SLEEPING BAGS

Use a heavy, down-filled sleeping bag in cold weather. In order for the bag to effectively keep you warm, the down must remain dry so store your sleeping bag inside a waterproof cover. A cotton liner allows an insulating layer between your body and the bag. Place a waterproof camping pad underneath the bag to protect against the cold, wet ground.

SNOW SHELTERS

Getting out of the wind is a priority if you intend to stay warm and survive. With any shelter you build, take care that it is ventilated. Never fall asleep in a snow shelter with a stove or lamp burning. Carbon monoxide poisoning is a very real danger in enclosed shelters.

Natural hollow

Dig the snow out from around the base of a tree, piling the snow up around the edges to form a wall that will block winds. When you build a fire for warmth, position it so it will not melt snow on the overhanging branches or set the branches on fire.

Igloo

Using a snow saw or large knife, cut out blocks of hard snow. The blocks should measure 1m (3ft) long, 40cm (15in) high and 20cm (8in) deep. The base of your igloo is a circle of blocks built round the hole left by your block cutting. Trim the top of this first layer so it spirals gently upwards. Continue to add layers of blocks, building up the walls and overlapping the blocks. Shape the blocks so they lean slightly inwards, forming a dome. Dig a hole beneath the wall that will double as an entrance and an area to trap cold air. Add several blocks along one inside wall to serve as a sleeping platform. The final cap block has to be larger than the hole so you can shape it with your knife and fit it exactly to the hole from the inside. You must cut ventilation holes in the walls. As your body heat warms the interior of the igloo, the surface of the inner walls will melt and freeze over, closing up gaps between the blocks.

Snow cave

If building an igloo is beyond your means, a snow cave is the next best thing. Locate a large snowdrift that has been packed down by wind. Hollow out a shelter and build a sleeping platform inside. Block the entrance with snow. Be certain to poke a hole or two to vent your snow cave. Check that your ventilation holes do not become blocked.

Snow trench

A snow trench can be constructed quickly as an emergency shelter. Cut a trench deep enough to protect you from the winds.

Snow caves

Dig into a packed snowdrift and excavate a cave. Use a snow block to block the entrance once inside. Be sure to poke at least one ventilation hole in the wall to prevent carbon monoxide poisoning. If available, a candle will help warm the interior.

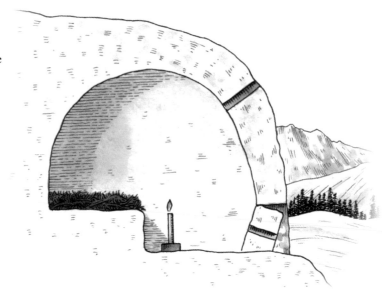

Create a platform on which you can sleep within the cave. It should be above the entrance to help protect against drafts. Line the platform with foliage to insulate yourself from the snow. Keep your digging tools inside the cave with you in case you need to dig yourself out again.

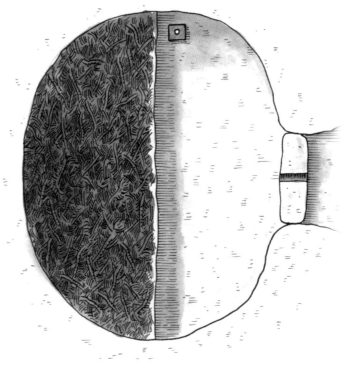

Snow trench

Cut a trench deep, long, and wide enough in which to lie comfortably. Insulate the bottom with a layer of foliage. A roof may be constructed by leaning snow blocks you've cut against one another in an A-shape. This shelter is quick to construct in emergencies and keeps winds out.

Insulate it with any foliage you can find. An A-frame roof can be constructed by leaning snow blocks against each other over the trench.

Lean-to

Lean-tos serve best in less windy situations. If branches and foliage are available, a simple shelter can be constructed in the form of a lean-to. Cut a long, straight branch and use it as the ridgepole. Try to make the ridgepole from a branch that is more than 60cm (2ft) taller than you. Trim off all the twigs. Cut two more sticks to chest height and lash them together at one end so they form an A-shape. This will function at one end of the lean-to.

Lash one end of the ridgepole to the A-shaped support and the other end to a tree trunk. Cut about half a dozen more branches long enough to lean at a 45° angle from the ground to the ridgepole. Layer saplings, boughs or foliage as a roof.

COLD INJURIES

Hypothermia, frostbite, immersion foot and dehydration are dangerous cold-related injuries. Their prevention, symptoms and treatment are described in Chapter 6.

Another health danger heavy snow presents is snow blindness. Snow blindness temporarily renders your pupils incapable of closing. The sun's ultra-violet rays reflecting

Lean-to

If in a wooded environment, you'll have all the
materials to build a lean-to. Constructed from
a long ridgepole, several sticks, foliage, and
lashing, the lean-to is a good shelter in less
windy conditions.

off of the snow into the eyes causes symptoms including temporary blindness, bloodshot eyes, sensitivity to light, severe headaches, the sensation of grit in the eyes and pain. If not treated it can lead to permanent eye damage. The treatment for snow blindness is bandaging the eyes and avoiding bright light until the symptoms subside.

To prevent snow blindness, wear sunglasses or snow goggles. If you lose your eye protection, you can improvise sunglasses from various materials. Cut slits in a piece of cardboard or bark from a tree and wear them as sunglasses. Even a strip of dark negative film can serve as sunglasses in an emergency. Smearing soot or charcoal beneath your eyes can help cut down glare.

TRAVEL ACROSS SNOW

- Do not travel during a blizzard.
- Use snowshoes when travelling across deep snow. Trudging through deep snow leads to exhaustion and can cause immersion foot.
- If crossing snowy ground in a group, walk single file within arm's reach of one another. This will prevent any member of your party from being lost.
- Use an ice axe as a walking stick and probe for hidden holes or crevasses.

DRIVING IN SNOW

- Before starting out, turn on the engine and run the heater and defroster.
- Use a scraper, not your windscreen (windshield) wipers, to clear the windscreen (windshield) of ice and snow.
- Clear any snow off of the vehicle.
- Remove snow that has built up immediately around the tyres (tires). Chunks of frozen snow that fall from the wheel wells while driving are a hazard.
- When starting out, accelerate gently so you do not lose traction.
- Always wear your seat belt while driving.
- Slow down and triple the distance

Types of avalanche

Wet slab avalanches are composed of snow mixed with water from spring thaws or rain. Though slow-moving, they destroy everything in their paths. Hard slab avalanches move at a higher speed and consist of enormous chunks that break off from old snow that is wind-compacted. Soft slab avalanches are the fastest moving and consist of billowing clouds of powder that plummet down the mountain.

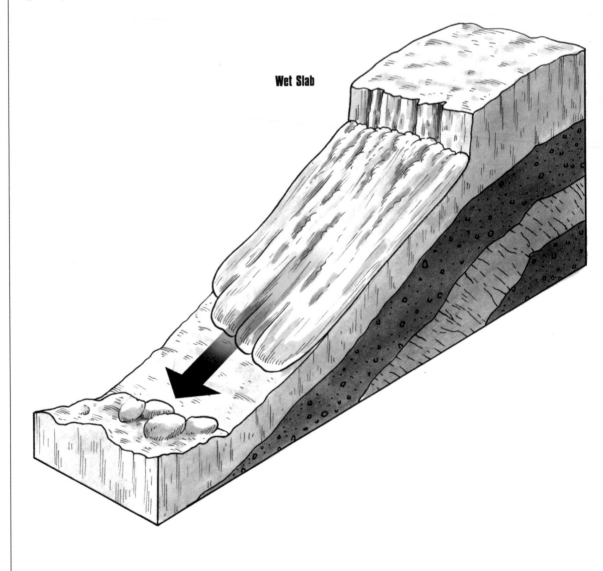

Wet Slab

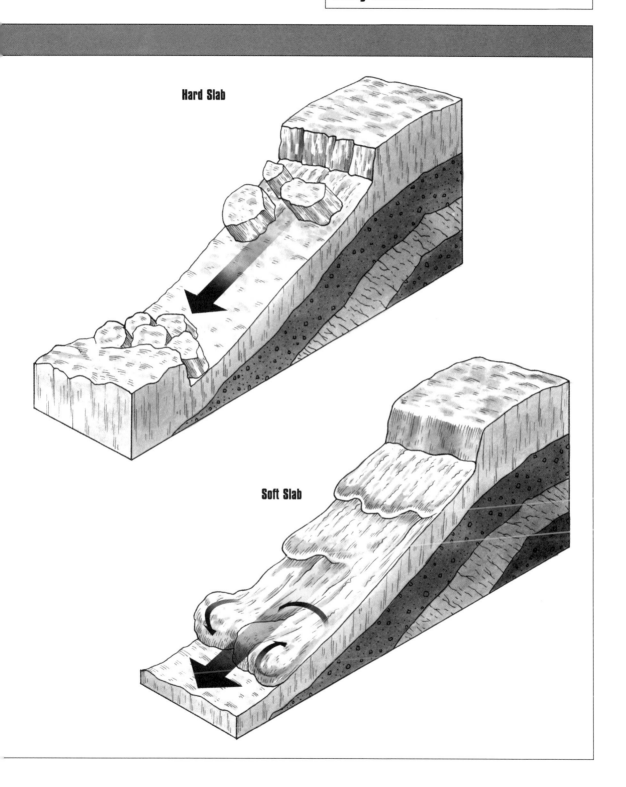

Hard Slab

Soft Slab

between you and the vehicle ahead of you.

- Change lanes and proceed through intersections with great caution.
- Stay in the ploughed (plowed) lane. Avoid driving over the ridges between the ploughed (plowed) areas. If you must change lanes, do so slowly.
- Drive with your headlamps (headlights) on. This makes it easier for other vehicles to see you.
- Keep windows, mirrors and lights free of ice or snow.
- If your vehicle has anti-lock brakes, press the brake pedal and hold it there. Do not pump the brakes.
- If you do not have anti-lock brakes and your brakes lock, remove your foot from the brake pedal for a moment.
- If you begin to skid on a slick surface, steer into the skid. For example, if the back end of your vehicle begins skidding to the left, turn the steering wheel to the left.
- Do not spin the tyres (tires). This heats the snow and creates a very slippery layer of water between the tyres (tires) and snow.
- If you must drive during a winter weather advisory or winter storm watch, travel during daylight, do not travel alone, stay on the main roads and be sure someone knows what route you are taking.
- Avoid driving during a winter storm warning.
- Do not drive during a blizzard. Pull over to the side of the road and turn on your hazard flashers.
- Keep your fuel tank full. This will prevent ice from forming in the tank or fuel lines.
- Monitor your radio for the most recent reports on road conditions.

AVALANCHES

Thousands of avalanches occur every winter and most of them are triggered by human activity. An avalanche occurs when an enor-

Avalanche protection

Though avalanches cannot be stopped, many avalanche-prone areas have installed barriers to slow them. Whether a natural barrier, such as trees, is used, or a man-made structure, the aim is to reduce the avalanche's impact on human lives.

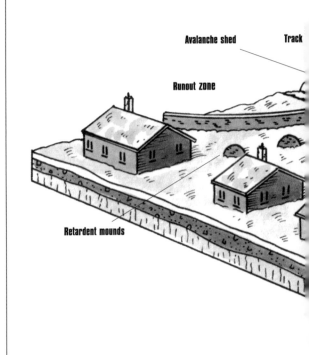

Avalanche shed   Track

Runout zone

Retardent mounds

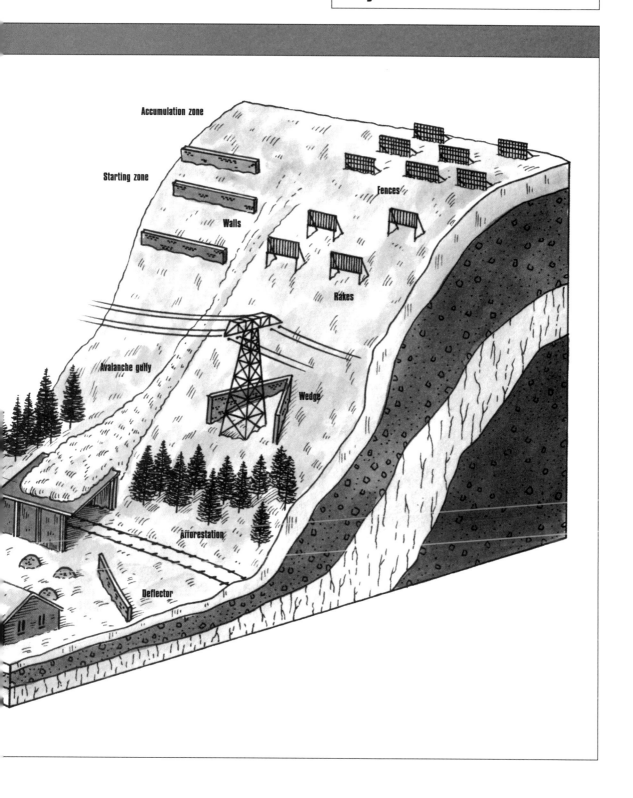

mous layer of snow is loosened and slides downhill. The setting for an avalanche involves a steep slope, snow cover, a weakened layer in the snow cover and a trigger, such as a skier or snowboarder.

Three primary avalanche types

Wet slab

Warming temperatures cause snow to weaken and slip down the slope. These avalanches are usually composed of snow mixed with rainwater. The snow spreads as it slides slowly down the mountain. While these avalanches tend to travel at speeds of only about 32 kilometres (20 miles) per hour, their danger lies in the enormous weight of the snow. This type of avalanche can uproot trees, carry along huge boulders and flatten structures in its paths. When it comes to a rest, buried victims cannot move or breathe because the snow settles like concrete.

Hard slab

The most common type of avalanche, the hard slab is composed of old snow that has been compacted by the wind. The top layer breaks into large, rock-hard chunks that travel down the slope at 48–80 kilometres (30–50 miles) per hour.

Soft slab

Also referred to as a powder avalanche, these occur when a layer of snow breaks away, charging down the slope like a dense cloud. This type of avalanche can travel at speeds up to 400 kilometres (250 miles) per hour and demolishes everything in its path.

SURVIVING AN AVALANCHE

- You cannot outrun an avalanche. If an avalanche barrier is available, use it for shelter.
- If caught in an avalanche, try to make your way to the surface or the edge of the flow by swimming.

- As the avalanche slows, beat the snow around you with your hands and legs to create an air space.
- Lie still and determine if you can see

Surviving an avalanche

If overtaken by an avalanche, try to stay on top of the flow and make it to the edge by making swimming motions. As soon as the flow stops, it will harden. As you feel the avalanche slow, flail with your arms and legs. This will create breathing space around you.

light. You may have landed close enough to the surface of the flow to easily dig yourself out.

● Allow saliva to dribble from your mouth

to help you discern which direction is up. The saliva will dribble downwards so the opposite direction is the way out.

● Remember that 50 per cent of avalanche

Base for signal fire

It may be necessary to build a base for a signal fire in a snow-covered area to prevent melting snow from extinguishing the flames. Use green logs to make a dry base for the fire. Lay several of these logs side by side to form the base. Arrange another layer on top of that one in the opposite direction. Build your fire on top of this base.

victims who survive free themselves.

- Carrying a beacon gives you an 80 per cent chance of being found if buried.
- Shout for help only if you hear rescuers very nearby. Snow muffles sound and you cannot be heard from far away.
- If you witness someone being caught in an avalanche, follow their movement with your eyes for as long as possible. Try to estimate where they landed when the flow ceased. Do not enter flow of snow while it is still moving to attempt a rescue. Wait until the avalanche stops.
- Always check local reports on avalanche conditions before going onto the slopes.

Survivor's story

When snowboarder Luke Edgar and his friend Gorio went snowboarding at Mount Ranier, Washington in 2001, Edgar was caught in an 'avy', or avalanche, and lived to tell his story.

'Everything was happening so fast and at the same time in slow motion. I didn't try to pull the ripcord that releases my board or take off my pack. Both would be anchors and all avy training says to ditch the gear. About this time the secondary wave of snow from above, which had a two- to three-foot [almost one metre] crown at its deepest point in a twenty-foot [6m]

wide section, hit me from behind with speed. This is the last time Gorio saw me as I was buried from this point on.

'I travelled the next 40-plus feet [12-plus m] face down thinking I would be going down a long way and not really knowing what was around the bend… I was still calm considering I was buried. I tried to reach my board to pull the rip-cord, but it was uphill. Before I knew it things were coming to a stop and I just managed to get my right hand in front of my face and my left hand about 10in [25cm] away.

'My goggles were still on and I could see; there was light. I tried to move, but the snow was cement. My body was stretched out to the fullest as my board was acting as an anchor with my body and pack being pulled downhill. My head was face down and well below my feet. I knew which way was up.

'I remembered Gorio did not have a transceiver…did he have his probe? I knew he had his shovel, but how deep was I? I know from experience that avy snow is cement and digging some-one out by yourself is com-pounded many times with each foot [0.3m] of snow that is on top of you… And if he doesn't have his probe, forget it. He has to have a

Clothing signals

You can create a signal flag from a shirt. Lash two sticks together in a T-shape and hang a shirt on them. Brighter colors that contrast with the landscape will draw attention. This improvised flag may be waved at search planes or placed in a clearing where it can be seen easily.

probe. We're in a hole, no one saw us and there was not enough time to get help. Fifteen minutes is all I have, all Gorio has to save me... I try to push again and bring my left hand closer to my face, which fills my little air pocket and mouth with snow, resulting in a double dose of panic.

'All I can think about is my family... I try to call out to Gorio again, but my breath has melted the snow, which is now starting to freeze around my head, greatly reducing the oxygen flow. Then I hear it, muffled and about ten feet [3m] or so away.

"Luke, Luke."

'It seemed like they only took ten seconds, could have been a minute, I don't know, but Gorio got my face free and I gasped for air screaming, 'You saved my life, you saved my life!' All I remember is feeling euphoric and telling Gorio how he saved my life. Gorio was moving fast as we were still in a very dangerous place. It took a minute to dig out my board and get it off my feet when Gorio accidentally knocked some snow in my face, blocking my breath. I yelled "Gorio, Gorio, my face!" as my arms and head were still locked in place. The helplessness was overwhelming.

'The strange thing was my goggles were not fogged, I guess the no-fog stuff I put on the inside and outside the night before worked and it was my brain that went dark.

'My head was pounding from the lack of oxygen. I had no more strength left but the thought of being ripped by another slide and being able to see my family again after giving up hope was more than enough motivation to climb out.'

SIGNALLING

When stranded in a snowy environment, it may be necessary to signal rescuers to indicate your location. Your signal must have maximum contrast against the snow to attract attention – movement also helps catch a rescuer's eye.

Fire

A signal fire works well at night, but it requires constant maintenance and must be protected from winds. You may need to build a platform of branches to keep melting snow from extinguishing your fire.

Smoke

During daylight, dark smoke against a background of white snow can draw attention. Adding rubber or oil-soaked rags to a fire can darken smoke. If the day is too windy, smoke will disperse and not be an effective way to signal.

Clothing

Brightly-coloured clothing or material spread on the snow will draw attention. You can also lash sticks together in a T-shape and hang a brightly coloured shirt on it as an improvised distress flag.

Natural material

You can use rocks, branches, brush or the snow itself to signal for rescue. You can tramp down snow in the shape of letters or symbols and fill them in with darker material such as twigs or branches.

If an aircraft approaches closely enough for the pilot to see you, signal using your body. The pilot will acknowledge having received and understood your message by rocking the plane from side to side. If the pilot has seen your signal but not understood, he will signal this by flying in a complete circle. Once the pilot has signalled your message has been received and understood, you can stop sending that signal. You may relay additional messages to the pilot via body signals once your original message has been acknowledged.

Sleeping in the cold

In cold conditions, you may feel the need to sleep as much as 12 hours. This is natural and is a way of conserving energy. Remember:

Signalling

If a rescue aircraft is close enough to see you,
use body signals to communicate.

Our receiver is operating

Affirmative (Yes)

Can proceed shortly, wait if practicable

Need mechhanical help or parts, long delay

Do not attempt to land here

Pick us up, aircraft abandoned

Use drop message

All OK, do not wait

Negative (No)

Land here (point in direction of landing)

Need medical assistance urgently

Plane signals

The pilot of the rescue plane indicates he has spotted you by maneuvering the plane and flashing lights. If your message was seen but not understood, the pilot will fly in a complete circle or flash red lights. If your message was seen and understood, the pilot will rock the wings from side to side or flash green lights.

Red flashes with signal lamp: MESSAGE RECEIVED AND NOT UNDERSTOOD

Green flashes with signal lamp: MESSAGE RECEIVED AND UNDERSTOOD

- Have plenty of fuel for your fire nearby.
- Be certain your shelter is windproof.
- Leave a signal to indicate your location in case rescuers come by while you're asleep.
- Place a layer of insulating material between your body and the ground
- Eat your largest meal just before you go to sleep.

- Wear extra clothing to bed.
- Do not forget to wear a hat.
- If some of your clothing is wet, remove it and place it in the cold to freeze. Once frozen, the ice can be removed by beating the material until it breaks off, leaving a dry garment.
- Plan the next day's activities if you cannot sleep.

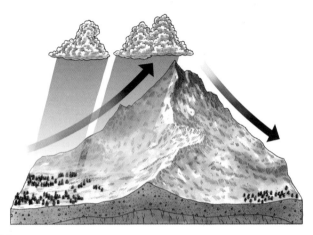

CHAPTER NINE

Extreme Environments

At sea and in the mountains, weather is a constant danger. It is especially important that you prepare for survival in these inhospitable environments. Safely negotiating rugged mountain terrain and meeting your basic needs while adrift necessitate specialized survival skills.

Two of the most inhospitable environments you can encounter are the open sea and mountains. There is little natural protection in either environment. You must be prepared to cope with extremes of temperature, wind, waves and dangerous terrain in order to survive.

AT SEA
Gear

When you board an aircraft or ocean-going vessel, familiarize yourself with the rescue and emergency gear they carry on board. Knowing where these items are stored can mean the difference between life and death.

- *Raft or dinghy*: usually made of rubber or tough canvas, these are normally inflatable. The best raft or dinghys are those with plenty of handles to grasp and a built-in canopy.
- *Flares*: hand-held, smoke and parachute flares improve your chances of being spotted by rescuers.
- *Strobe lights*: these compact signals are easily spotted at night and can be attached to your life raft or life jacket.
- *Cord*: sturdy nylon cord will come in handy and can be used in many situations.
- *Sea anchor (drogue)*: can be used to control drifting.

- *Waterproof containers*: used to hold food, waterproof matches, flares and maps.
- *Gaff and net*: absolutely necessary for catching fish at sea. It is important to make sure that the point of the gaff should remain embedded in cork when not in use to prevent punctures to the raft or your skin.

In the water

Your chances of survival in the water are dependent upon a number of factors:

- Your survival chances increase if you are in a life raft.
- The temperature of the water affects how long you will be able to survive if you are afloat without a raft.
- Your survival chances increase if you are afloat in warm water, but tropical waters bring the threat of dangerous sea creatures.

Do not abandon a ship unless it is too dangerous to remain on board. Even a damaged ship can provide shelter and survival supplies. It will also be easier for rescuers to spot you in a disabled ship than in a tiny life raft.

Jumping into the water

Avoid jumping into the water if you can. Instead, climb down into the water if at all possible. When faced with no choice but to jump, first make sure the water you are jumping into is clear of people or debris. Check that your life jacket is fastened securely round your body, but not yet inflated. When jumping, keep your back straight and your body vertical. Fold your arms and cross your ankles. Cover your mouth and pinch your nose shut with one hand. Shut your eyes and jump from the lowest point possible.

Once in the water, inflate your life jacket. Find your way to a life raft or look for a large piece of floating debris to cling to. If there is nothing to cling to, relax and float. Humans are extremely buoyant in salty water. You should only try to swim in warm water and then only to reach a flotation aid or land that is very nearby.

If you were in an aircraft that went down at sea, stay in the vicinity of the aircraft, but keep a safe distance. If you remain too close, you could be pulled underwater by the vortex created by the sinking fuselage. If fuel or oil is floating on the water, move away from it. If you are close to an area where oil or fuel is burning on the water's surface, do not inflate your life jacket. First swim underwater as far as possible to clear the burning area. When surfacing for a breath, make wide, sweeping movements with your hands to disperse any burning material on the surface. Repeat this process until you are in safer water. Then inflate your life jacket.

Improvising a flotation device

A flotation device is necessary even for the strongest

Human survival times in the sea

Water Temperature		Exhaustion/	Expected Time
°F	°C	Unconsciousness	of Survival
32.5	0.3	15 minutes	15-45 minutes
32.5-40	0.3-4.4	15-30 minutes	30-90 minutes
40-50	4.4-10	30-60 minutes	1-3 hours
50-60	10-15.6	1-2 hours	1-6 hours
60-70	15.6-21.1	2-7 hours	2-40 hours
70-80	21.1-26.7	3-12 hours	3 hours - indefinitely
80	26.7	indefinitely	indefinitely

(Source: NOAA)

swimmers. It helps to keep your head above water so that you can breathe easily and also so that your body heat is not lost to the water.

A pair of trousers can be fashioned into a flotation device. Tie the trouser legs together at the ankles. While treading water with your legs, you can use your teeth to tighten the knot. Grasp the trousers by the belt or waistband and throw them forwards

Heat-Escape-Lessening Posture (HELP)

When floating in cold water it is essential that you conserve body heat. Cross your arms across your chest and draw your knees up to help maintain your core body temperature. This position is known as the Heat-Escape-Lessening Posture (HELP).

Heat Loss Areas

Keep your shoes and clothing on and your head and shoulders above water to conserve body heat. There are several areas of the body that lose heat. Assuming the Heat-Escape-Lessening Posture helps retain body heat.

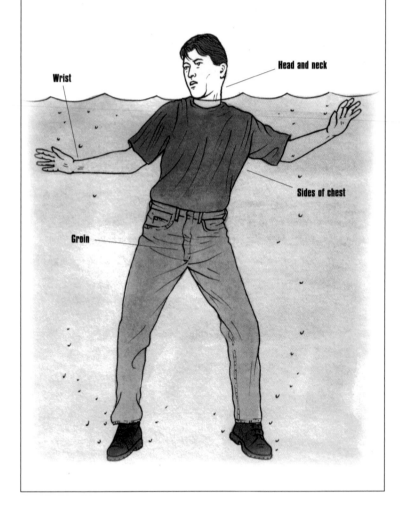

Wrist

Head and neck

Sides of chest

Groin

Floating

Cold water survival

It is better to remain still and float than to try swimming because swimming expends valuable body heat. You can gather debris and hold it to your chest to help you float if you do not have a life jacket. Most of your body heat is lost through the head, neck, wrists, groin and sides of the chest. Keep all your clothes on including your shoes. They will help keep you warm. Assume the heat-escape-lessening posture (HELP) to conserve body

over your head, scooping as much air into them as possible. Put your head between the trouser legs and hold the waist closed below the water's surface. Remove the trousers from around your neck and scoop in more air as needed.

Your body will naturally float just below the water's surface. Relax your body and tread water with your legs. Exhale with your face under water as you scoop downwards with your hands and raise your head above the sur-face. Take a deep breath once your lungs are empty. Holding your breath, put your face back in the water and relax, allowing your legs to float behind you. Repeat this process when you need another breath.

heat by folding your arms, drawing your knees up to your chest and crossing your ankles. This will conserve heat in your abdomen and help maintain your core body temperature. The heat-escape-lessening pos-ture can prolong your survival time by up to 50 per cent.

If there are others with you, huddle together to share body heat. Place any chil-dren in the centre of the huddle. Do not fall asleep and do not allow anyone in your group to fall asleep. You must fight the urge to sleep and remain alert, keeping an eye out for rescuers.

Rafts

Some life rafts inflate upside down. A rope is attached so you can right the raft. To right an upside-down life raft in choppy water you must do the following:

- Manoeuvre to the side of the raft where the pull rope is located.
- Pull yourself up onto the edge of the raft in a kneeling position.
- Brace against the raft by pulling backwards on the rope, then stand up.
- Keeping your feet on the edge of the raft, fall backwards into the water.

Improvising a float

Tie trouser (pant) legs together at the ankle, using your teeth to tighten the knot as you tread water with your legs. Scoop air into the trousers by throwing the open trousers over your head. Place your head between the trouser legs and hold the waist shut beneath the water's surface. Repeat when trousers lose air.

● As the far side of the raft rises, continue pulling on the rope. If there is more than one life raft in the area, use cord to lash them together. It will be easier for rescuers searching for survivors to spot a larger object in the water. Tie a lifeline

calm. Windy conditions can cause hazardous waves.

Drinking water

As in any other survival situation, the priority is to conserve body fluids and procure additional water. If your life raft contains a still, set it up as soon as you are situated in the raft. A tarp can be stretched across the raft for catching rainwater. Arrange the tarp across the raft at night like a canopy, turning up the edges to create a hem that will collect dew.

- Do not drink seawater. It can cause kidney failure.
- Do not drink alcohol. It will accelerate dehydration.

Food

Water is a much higher priority than food at sea. The digestion process depletes precious body fluids. Of course, fish are abundant at sea, and fishing can help break up the monotony of being adrift. Be careful with your fishing equipment. Hooks can injure you or puncture the life raft. Lines can also cut into your hands and damage the raft. If sharks are in the area, do not fish. Remember too that fish entrails in the water can attract sharks.

Floating seaweed is edible, but it has a laxative effect. Eat only small amounts to avoid dehydration.

ILLNESS AT SEA

As if being cast adrift is not ordeal enough, being at the mercy of the elements makes you vulnerable to various ailments.

Seasickness

Characterized by nausea and vomiting, seasickness is caused by the motion of the life raft. It can result in extreme fluid loss, exhaustion and the loss of the will to survive. The vomit can attract sharks and

from yourself to the raft. Put out your anchor immediately to avoid drifting. With any luck, the sea will be relatively

Huddle together

In cold water, huddle closely together to conserve heat. In a group you are also more visible to rescuers. Chests should be touching if possible. Small children should be placed at the centre of the huddle. It is important that everyone remain awake.

make other survivors retch. In cases of seasickness, the victim should wash any vomit off of the raft. Do not allow the sufferer to eat until the nausea subsides. Advise the victim to lie down and rest. Administer seasickness pills if they are available. Using the horizon as a focal point can help overcome seasickness.

Wave heights

Force	Wind Speed		Sea Terms	Height of Waves	
	In Knots	Km/hour		Meters	Feet
0	under 1	Under 1	calm	0	0
1	1–3	1–5	smooth	less than 0.3	less than 1
2	4–6	6–11	slight	0.3–0.9	1–3
3	7–10	12–19	moderate	0.9–1.5	3–5
4	11–16	20–28	rough	1.5–2.4	5–8
5	17–21	29–38	rough	1.5–2.4	5–8
6	22–27	39–49	rough	1.5–2.4	5–8
7	28–33	50–61	very rough	2.4–3.7	8–12
8	34–40	62–74	very rough	2.4–3.7	8–12
9	41–47	75–88	high	3.7–6.1	12–20
10	48–55	89–102	very high	6.1–12.2	20–40
11	56–63	103–117	mountainous	12.2 and higher	40 and higher
12	64 +	118 +	confused		

Saltwater sores

Long-term exposure to seawater can produce a body rash or boils, which can turn septic. Any small break in the skin will become infected and turn into pus-filled sores. These sores should be drained, cleaned with fresh water, if available, and treated with antiseptic from the first aid kit. Bathing and washing your clothes in rainwater during a downpour can help prevent saltwater sores. While wetting your clothing in seawater can help keep your body cool, you run the risk of developing saltwater sores.

Dehydration

Prolonged exposure to the sun and reduced fluid intake can lead to dehydration. Vomiting, diarrhoea and sweating accelerate its effects. You must drink water regularly, stay out of the sun and conserve energy to avoid dehydration.

Sunburn

Not only does the sun beat down on you from above, the water reflects the sun's rays back up at you. While it is difficult to avoid a certain amount of sunburn at sea, you must make an effort to limit it. Apply sun block liberally and wear clothing that covers as much skin as possible. Do not forget to apply sun block to the backs of your ears and your eyelids. Rig a sunshade or canopy on your life raft to protect you.

Hypothermia

Hypothermia is a concern if you have spent any amount of time in cold water. Use the heat-escape-lessening posture to conserve body heat if you are floating. In a life raft, huddle with others or bundle up in a foil emergency blanket to warm yourself.

Sea creatures

If you are afloat in tropical waters, your chances of survival are far greater than in cold waters. However, tropical waters contain a wide variety of biting or stinging sea life. If you encounter a fish you are uncertain about, treat it with caution. Any fish that are spiny or box-shaped should not be eaten or touched.

If stung by a sea creature, apply a tourniquet between the wound and your heart. You can release the tourniquet after about 10 minutes. A mild acid, such as lemon juice or vinegar, applied round the wound will neutralize the venom. Use tweezers, not bare hands, to remove any tentacles or spines embedded in your flesh.

Sharks

Most varieties of sharks are not aggressive and do not attack. However, they will investigate anything unusual in the water. If you remain calm and still while they investigate, they will likely swim away once they are convinced you are not one of their usual food sources. Blood in the water will attract sharks and cause them to attack. For this reason you should not shoot or injure a shark as an attempt to scare it off. A bleeding shark will attract more sharks.

- Do not make noise or splash around. Sharks are extremely sensitive to vibrations in the water.
- Use shark repellent if you have it, and stay in the repellent-stained water.
- Remove watches or shiny jewellery. They

Righting a life raft

Often life rafts inflate upside down. Using the pull rope, pull yourself into a kneeling position on the raft's edge. Pulling backwards on the rope, stand up. As you keep your feet on the raft's edge and fall backwards into the water, the far side of the raft will rise. Continue to pull on the rope as you fall into the water; this will flip the raft over upright.

may look like a small fish to a shark.

- Do not empty your entire bladder at once. Sharks can be attracted by urine in the water. Urinate in small amounts, allowing the urine to dissipate before urinating again.
- If the need to vomit arises, do so in your hand and throw it as far away from you as you can.
- When floating in a raft, do not let your arms or legs hang over the edge and trail in the water.
- If a shark actually does attack you, kick and thrash at the shark, hitting its eyes

and gills. It may decide you are not worth the trouble.

A SURVIVOR'S STORY

After his sailboat the *Napoleon Solo* capsized in the Atlantic Ocean, American naval architect Steven Callahan was lost at sea for 76 days, adrift in a life raft called the *Rubber Ducky III*. More than 70 days into his ordeal he writes about improvising a water collection device to replace his damaged solar still.

'I stick with the routine that I've followed for two and a half months. At night I take a look around each time I awaken.

Every half-hour during the day, I stand and carefully peruse the horizon in all directions. I have done this more than two thousand times now. Instinctively I know how the waves roll, when one will duck and weave to give a clear view for another 300ft (90m) or almost half a mile (800m). This noon a freighter streams up from astern, a bit to the north of us. The hand flares are nearly invisible in the daylight, so I choose an orange smoke flare and pop it. The dense orange genie spreads its arms out and flies off downwind just above the water. Within 100ft (30m) it has been blown into a haze thinner than the smoke of a crowded pub. The ship cuts up the Atlantic a couple of miles abeam and smoothly steams off to the west. She must be headed to an island port.

'I work all the rest of the day and all of the morning of April 19 to create an elaborate water-collection device. Using the aluminium tubing from the radar reflector and my last dead solar still, I make Rubber Ducky *a bonnet that I secure to the summit of the canopy arch tube. The half circle of aluminium tubing keeps the face of the bonnet (hood) open and facing aft. A bridle adjusts the angle of the face, which I keep nearly vertical, and the wind blows the bonnet (hood) forwards like a bag. I fit a drain and tubing that I can run inside to fill up containers while I tend to the other water collectors.*

'For hours I watch white, fluffy cumulus rise up from the horizon and slowly pass. Sometimes they band together and form dense herds running in long lines. Those that have grazed over the Atlantic long enough grow thick and muscular, rearing up to great billowing heights, churning violently, their underbellies flat and black. When they can hold no more, their rain thunders down in black streaks that lash the sea. I chew upon

dried sticks of dorado awaiting the test of my new tools.

'But it seems that the paths of the squalls are bound to differ from mine. Sometimes a long line of clouds passes close by. I watch the wispy edges swirl above me and feel a few drops or a momentary sprinkle coming down. It's just enough to show me that my new water collection gear is very effective. I'm convinced that I'll collect several pints [litres], maybe even a gallon [a few litres], if I can just get directly in the path of a single heavy shower. It's one thing to have a tool and quite another to be in a position to use it. My eyes wander from the horizon to the sky. I'm so tired of always awaiting something.'

The Beaufort Scale can be used at sea to estimate wind speeds based on the appearance of the sea.

SIGNALLING AT SEA

The vastness of the ocean makes sea rescue especially challenging. Do not use consumable signalling devices unless a plane or ship is near. You can regularly sweep the horizon with a heliograph, or mirror, even when help is not in sight. Doing so will keep you occupied and alert, and it will alleviate boredom.

- A camera flash can be used to signal, but overusing it will deplete the battery.
- At night a red parachute flare can be seen for about 11km (7 miles). These flares reach a height of about 91m (300ft).
- A red hand-held flare can be tied to the end of a paddle or held aloft as high as possible in your hand. Visible for about 5km (3 miles), it is best used at night.
- During the day, orange smoke is an effective signal, provided there is no wind or at least it is relatively calm and

conditions are clear.

- If an aircraft or ship is within sight, you can carefully stand up in the life raft and signal with your arms.
- Anti-collision white flares should only be used when all other flares have been used up. This type of flare is most visible at night or at close range, they are normally used to reduce the risk of collisions with other vessels.

SIGNS OF LAND

While adrift, keep an eye out for signs of nearby land. Cumulus clouds in a clear sky form over land and can be spotted long before the land itself is in view. Animals can also give clues to the location of land-masses. Flocks of seabirds normally stay within 100km (62 miles) of land. In the morning they will be flying away from land. In the afternoon they will be returning to shore. Spotting a seal means land is near because seals do not venture far from shore. In the ocean, deep water is dark in colour. Shallower water near shore is a lighter colour.

The Beaufort Scale used at sea

Beaufort Number	Speed (mph)	Speed (kph)	Description	Effects at sea
0	< 1	< 1	Calm	sea like a mirror
1	2–3	1–5	Light air	ripples with appearance of 'fish scales'; no foam crests
2	4–7	6–11	Light breeze	small wavelets; crests of glassy appearance not breaking
3	8–12	12–19	Gentle breeze	large wavelets; crests begin to break; scattered whitecaps
4	13–18	20–29	moderate breeze	small waves, becoming longer; numerous whitecaps
5	19-24	30-38	fresh breeze	moderate waves, becoming longer; many whitecaps; some spray
6	25–31	39–51	strong breeze	larger waves forming; whitecaps everywhere; more spray
7	32–38	51-61	near gale	sea heaps up; white foam from breaking waves begins to be blown in streaks
8	39–46	62–74	gale	moderately high waves of greater length; foam is blown in well-marked streaks
9	47-54	75-86	strong gale	high waves, sea begins to roll; dense streaks of foam; spray reduces visibility
10	55-63	87-101	whole gale	very high waves with overhanging crests; sea takes white appearance
11	64-74	102–120	storm	exceptionally high waves; sea covered with white foam patches
12	> 74	> 120	hurricane force	air filled with foam; sea completely white with driving spray

Rain-shadow effect

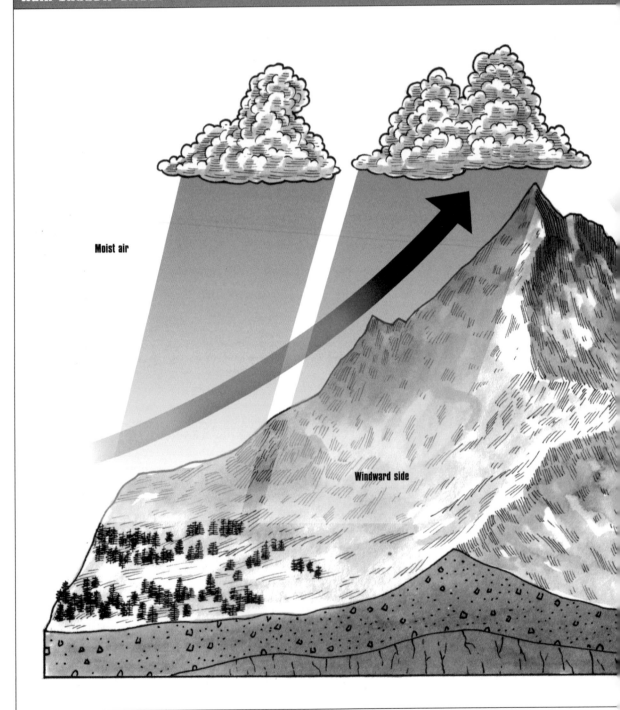

Moist air

Windward side

Mountains experience the rain-shadow effect. The windward slope is associated with rising air, clouds, and precipitation. The leeward slope experiences descending air and dry conditions.

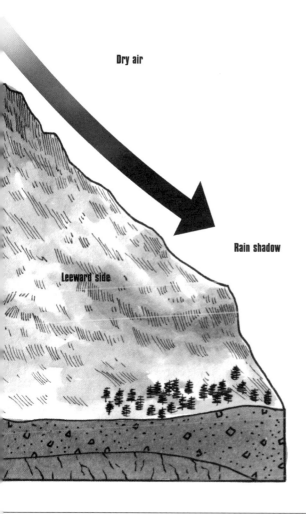

Dry air

Rain shadow

Leeward side

Atmospheric pressure change

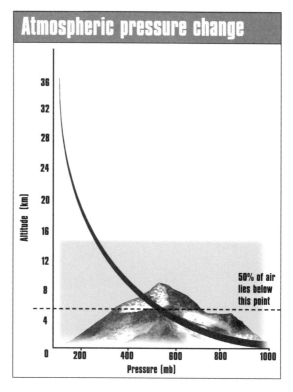

50% of air lies below this point

Altitude (km)

Pressure (mb)

IN THE MOUNTAINS
Gear

Before venturing into mountainous areas, certain pieces of equipment are required to negotiate the rough terrain.

- An ice axe is an essential tool for walking on steep slopes or icy terrain. Secure the axe to your belt so it cannot be lost.
- Ski poles can be used for support when walking on snow or ice.
- Warm clothing should be worn in layers as described in Chapter 6.
- Sunglasses or goggles will prevent snow blindness.
- A down-filled, mummy-style sleeping bag will keep you warm while asleep.
- An insulating mat provides a layer between your sleeping bag and the cold ground.

Hiking uphill

When hiking uphill, take shorter steps
and keep the same rhythm. Lean forward
and place your feet flat on the ground to
maintain balance.

Survival procedures

In the rugged terrain of a mountain it is easy to become disoriented. If you become lost in the mountains:

- Stop and calmly assess your situation. Unless you are absolutely certain of the path you took to get there, do not try to retrace your steps.
- If separated from a group, stay put. This will make it easier for them to find you.
- Whistle or shout occasionally and listen quietly for a response before trying again.
- If you move, use rocks to arrange arrows on the ground to indicate the direction you are travelling.
- Use your ice axe or pole to test for hidden crevasses.
- Seek shelter in a cave or overhang if conditions are extremely cold or wet. Leave a clearly marked trail in case rescuers come by while you are in the shelter.
- If it is windy, put on your windproof, waterproof jacket before you feel chilled.
- Do not move about if it is snowing heavily.

Rain-shadow effect

Weather conditions can differ greatly at different places on the mountain. As an air mass approaches a mountain, the air rises and cools.

Clouds form on the windward side, which is the side facing the wind. Precipitation usually results from these windward side clouds. As the air mass crosses the summit, it descends the leeward, or downwind, side of the mountain. This descending air heats up, leading to drier conditions on the leeward

Hiking downhill

Lean back slightly when descending a hill. Descending a hill is more strenuous on the knees than ascending, so do not try to walk too quickly.

Manteling

Place both elbows on the overhang and keep your chest against the rock. Lift one ankle onto the overhang while leaning on your elbows. Move your knee onto the overhang as you push your body upwards with your hands.

side of the mountain. The drier leeward side of the mountain experiences what is called the rain-shadow effect.

ALTITUDE ILLNESSES

Altitude sickness is an illness that occurs primarily at altitudes above 2440m (8000ft). It is caused by lowered oxygen intake, which is the result of the thinner air that exists at higher altitudes.

Acute Mountain Sickness (AMS)

There are severarl symptoms of acute mountain sickness. They include headache, dizziness, fatigue, nausea, shortness of breath, blue lips, decreased appetite and clumsiness. The best way to treat AMS is to drink plenty of fluids, reduce your activity level and allow several days to acclimatize. In severe cases, descend to below 900m (3000ft).

High-Altitude Cerebral Oedema (HACE)

At altitudes above 3660m (12,000ft), oxygen starvation can cause the brain to swell. Poor coordination, persistent headaches, plus all the symptoms of AMS characterize this disorder. Anyone suffering from HACE must immediately be removed to a lower altitude and treated for 12 hours with oxygen.

MOUNTAIN HIKING

When walking uphill, do not take long strides. Take shorter steps and maintain a rhythm. Lean forwards and place your feet flat on the ground. When descending, lean back slightly and do not try to proceed too quickly. Use a pole or walking stick for support because descending is particularly hard on the knees.

Basic Climbing Techniques

While serious rock climbing should be left to those with training, with a few basic climbing techniques you can overcome barriers and descend mountainous terrain safely. A survival situation is not the proper time to teach yourself advanced climbing techniques. Remember to avoid loose rocks, snowfields, glaciers and overhanging snow. When climbing without a rope, always maintain three points of contact.

Look for the easiest, safest route. Always look around and up. Do not over-stretch; use small movements and descend or ascend gradually. Think ahead several moves and plan your path. Seek out handholds and footholds above you in case you get stuck and have to reverse your direction. Lower yourself carefully and do not stand on tiptoe. Let your legs support most of your weight. When stuck, try a different route.

Manteling

This method is used for pulling yourself up on bulges in the rock face. It is a move rather like hauling yourself up out of a swimming pool.

High-Altitude Pulmonary Oedema (HAPE)

HAPE is brought on by exertion at high altitudes and oxygen deprivation. It has the same symptoms as AMS plus a dangerous fluid build-up in the lungs. Shortness of breath will continue even when at rest. You must descend below 900m (3000ft) and treat the condition with oxygen. A victim of HAPE will require three to four recovery days.

Chimneying

In the rock cleft, brace yourself by pushing outwards with your legs and hands. Place one foot firmly against the back wall and the hand on the same side of your body against the front wall.

Push upwards with your legs as you move your back up the wall.

Because chimneying is so strenuous, you must frequently rest. Lean back against the wall with your legs and arms straight and give your muscles a chance to recover.

- Pull yourself up until you can brace your elbows on the overhang.
- Keep your chest close to the rock and lean on one elbow.
- Throw one leg up and hook an ankle onto the overhang.
- Push down with both hands while moving your knee onto the overhang.
- Push yourself up onto the overhang.

Chimneying

The method for climbing between two rocks is called chimneying. Make sure the opening between the two rocks is large enough to accommodate your entire body. Look up the rock face and plan your route before you begin.

- Brace your back and hands against one rock face, and your feet against the opposite rock to begin.

- Press one foot against the rear wall and the hand on the same side of your body against the front wall.
- Push with your legs to move your back and buttocks up the wall.

Chimneying is strenuous, so you must rest regularly. To rest, lean back against the wall with your legs and arms straight in the same position you used to begin.

Survival instinct

Being faced with a survival situation in the open sea or mountains can seem especially hopeless. The very size of an ocean or a mountain can cause you to despair of ever being rescued. Though daunting situations, many others have survived them in the past. As long as you do not try anything rash and draw upon everything you have learned about survival, you too will prevail.

Glossary

air mass – body of air in which the temperature and humidity remain constant.

anticyclone – these are winds rotating outward from a high-pressure area, producing fair weather.

altitude – vertical elevation.

altocumulus – puffy, mid-level cloud composed of water vapour.

altostratus – layered, mid-level cloud composed of water vapour.

anemometer – an instrument with several rotating cups used to measure wind speed.

atmosphere – the mass of air surrounding the earth.

atmospheric pressure – this is simply the weight of air.

avalanche – rapid movement of a detached mass of snow and ice down a steep mountain slope.

barometer – instrument that measures atmospheric pressure.

beacon – a safety device that is carried on avalanche-prone slopes. It emits signals allowing rescuers to locate victims buried in the snow.

blizzard – a severe snowstorm with wind-driven snow and intense cold.

CFCs – chlorofluorocarbons. A group of synthetic gases that contribute to the depletion of the ozone layer.

chimneying – climbing or descending a gap between rocks by using the hands and feet for support on opposite sides of a fissure.

cholera – disease characterized by severe vomiting and dysentery.

cirrocumulus – high, thin, wispy clouds that appear in a patchy pattern.

cirrostratus – high, thin, wispy clouds that appear as whitish, translucent veils.

cirrus – wispy, feathery white clouds that appear at high altitudes.

climate – an average of daily weather conditions over an extended period of time.

cloud – visible accumulation of minute water droplets or ice crystals suspended in the air.

cold front – leading edge of a cool air mass that is actively displacing a warmer air mass

conduction – transfer of thermal energy by physical contact of two objects of differing temperatures.

convection – the process of heat transfer via the physical movement of a fluid from one place to another.

core – centre of the body, the temperature of which must be maintained to sustain life.

coriolis effect – the apparent deflection of free-moving objects, including winds and ocean currents, in response to the Earth's rotation. This deflection is to the right in the Northern Hemisphere and to the left in the Southern Hemisphere.

cumulonimbus – an anvil-shaped cumulus cloud extending to great heights, usually producing precipitation.

cumulus – puffy, white cloud that forms from columns of rising air.

cyclone – winds rotating into a low-pressure area, causing bad weather.

dehydration – excessive loss of body fluids.

doldrums – part of the ocean near the equator characterized by calm winds. Also called the Intertropical Convergence Zone.

drought – a long period of dry weather.

dysentery – this is a disorder that is marked by diarrhea with blood and mucus in the faeces.

El Niño – a warm ocean current that periodically appears off the coast of Peru and Ecuador, with wide-reaching environmental consequences.

Equator – the parallel of 0° latitude.

evaporation – the change of a substance from liquid to vapor.

exosphere – atmospheric layer extending 310 miles (499km) above the earth's surface, blending into interplanetary space.

eye – the calm centre of a tropical cyclone.

eye wall – zone at the edge of a tropical cyclone's eye where winds reach their highest speeds.

Ferrell Cells – two complete vertical circulation cells between the 30° and 60° latitudes, where air circulates between the Hadley Cells and Polar Cells.

flare – a distress signal used on land or at sea, in the form of a flame or light.

floodplain – area subject to periodic or episodic inundation.

front – the boundary or leading edge between air masses with differing temperatures.

frostbite – the freezing of body tissues. It can cause damage and, in extreme cases, death.

gaiters – protective fabric or plastic worn on lower legs to keep out moisture, dirt, or rocks.

gale – a strong wind.

gangrene – the dying of a body part due to interference with its nutrition.

Gulf Stream – a warm current, one of the major surface ocean currents.

greenhouse effect – an increase in greenhouse gases that retain heat in the Earth's atmosphere, resulting in a rise in global temperatures.

Hadley Cells – two complete vertical circulation cells between the equator where warm air rises, to 30° of latitude where most of the air subsides.

hail – precipitation in the form of small lumps of ice.

heat exhaustion – condition resulting from excessive exposure to heat, exertion, and lack of water.

heatstroke – condition in which the body becomes overheated, resulting in collapse.

heliograph – reflector used for signaling with the sun's rays.

HELP – Heat Escape Lessening Posture, used when floating in water to reduce loss of body heat.

humidity – the water vapor content of the air.

hurricane – tropical cyclone characterized by powerful thunderstorms and whirling winds, affecting North or Central America. May measure hundreds of miles in diameter.

hypothermia – potentially fatal condition in which core body temperature drops as a result of extended exposure to cold.

ice awls – pointed instruments for making small holes in ice.

igloo – dome-shaped shelter made from snow blocks.

immersion foot – also known as trench foot. This fungal condition of the skin is caused by excessive exposure to dampness.

ionosphere See thermosphere.

ITCZ (Intertropical Convergence Zone) See doldrums.

jet stream – two fast-moving streams of air that occur in the upper part of the troposphere.

landfall – the change in a tropical cyclone's path from over water to over land.

latitude – distance measured north and south of the equator.

layering – method of using layers of clothing to insulate.

lightning – flash of light produced by a discharge of atmospheric electricity.

longitude – distance measured east and west from the primer meridian on the earth's surface.

manteling – a rock climbing technique used to ascend or descend overhangs and bulges in a rock face.

mesosphere – atmospheric layer that extends 30–50 miles (48–80 km) above earth's surface.

meteorologist – scientist that studies the atmosphere and its phenomena, with an emphasis on weather and weather forecasting.

monsoon – a seasonal reversal of winds with distinctive seasonal rains.

mountain bibs – pants with suspenders and a high waistband, usually insulated.

nimbostratus – low, dark cloud, often appearing as widespread overcast, normally associated with precipitation.

northern hemisphere – the half of the earth north of the equator.

ozone layer – protective atmospheric layer which absorbs ultraviolet solar radiation.

permafrost – permanent ground ice or permanently frozen subsoil.

Polar Cells – areas of high pressure situated over both polar regions.

precipitation – water in liquid or solid form falling through the atmosphere to the earth's surface.

radiation – the process by which heat is emitted from a body.

rain – most common form of precipitation, consisting of drops of liquid water.

relative humidity – ratio of actual amount of water vapour in the air to maximum amount of water vapour the air could hold at that temperature and pressure.

sandstorm – a windstorm that drives clouds of sand.

snow – solid precipitation in the form of ice crystals, small pellets, or flakes.

snow blindness – a painful condition caused by excessive exposure to the sun's ultraviolet rays reflecting off of snow.

solar still – device used to distil contaminated water using the sun's heat.

southern hemisphere – the half of the earth south of the equator.

still – apparatus used to heat gas or vapour and condense it to liquid.

storm surge – the extremely high ocean water levels that accompany the landfall of a tropical cyclone.

stratosphere – atmospheric layer that contains the ozone layer, it extends six to thirty miles (10–48km) above earth's surface.

stratus – a cloud characterized by a gre horizontal layer

sunblock – cream or lotion barrier applied to the skin to protect against sunburn.

sunburn – skin inflammation caused by overexposure to sunlight.

sunspot – one of the dark spots that periodically appear on the sun's surface.

synoptic map – uses symbols to show weather conditions for a particular area, used by meteorologists to forecast weather.

teepee – cone-shaped structure built by leaning three or more sticks together.

temperature – the measure of thermal energy contained by an object or substance.

thermosphere – atmospheric layer extending 50 to 310 miles (80–499km) above earth's surface. Also called ionosphere.

thunderstorm – violent storm accompanied by thunder, lightning, and precipitation.

tinder – small, dry, combustible material used to start a fire.

tornado – dangerous storm characterized by whirling winds and a funnel-shaped cloud.

tropical cyclone – intense, revolving, destructive storm consisting of a low-pressure center.

tropic of Cancer – the parallel of 23° north latitude.

tropic of Capricorn – parallel of 23° south latitude.

troposphere – atmospheric layer that extends zero to six miles (0–10km) above earth's surface.

tropopause – uppermost limit of the troposphere.

typhoid – disease characterized by fever, diarrhea, and intestinal inflammation.

typhoon – term used for a tropical cyclone in the western North Pacific.

vent – to open clothing, zippers, or buttons to allow excess body heat to escape.

warm front – leading edge of an advancing warm air mass actively displacing colder air.

weather – short-term atmospheric conditions for a given time and a specific area.

weather satellite – a man-made object that orbits the earth, collecting images of cloud cover.

wind chill – a measure of how cold the combination of wind and cold feels to the human body, as opposed to a measure of air temperature alone.

SURVIVORS' STORIES

Lightning strike survival story, pp58–60
Source: Ely, Steve. 'Steve Ely's Story'. http://wvlightning.com/ststeve.html, 1998

Hail survival story, pp63–64
Source: Brewer, Gina Montgomery. 'The Storm'. http://members.tripod.com/~jalpanthers/g_storm.htm, 1998

Flood survival story, pp66–69
Source: Conn, Larry. 'Appalachian Coal Miners' True Stories'/ Dotson-Lewis, Betty. http://www.appalachianpower.com/Buffalo%20Creek%20Flood.htm, 2002

Hurricane survival story, pp78–79
Source: Frankovich, k.t. 'The Multifaceted k.t.'/Whittaker, Jeremy, http://members.aol.com/kfrnkovich/interview.html, 1999

Tornado survival story, pp90–94
Source: Felknor, Peter S. The Tri-State Tornado: The Story of America's Greatest Tornado Disaster. Ames: Iowa State University Press, 1992.

Frostbite survival story, pp113–115
Source: Fiennes, Ranulph. *Mind Over Matter: The Epic Crossing of the Antarctic Continent*. New York: Delacorte Press, 1993.

Extreme heat survival stiry, pp134–136
Source: Asher, Michael. *Two Against the Sahara*. New York: William Morrow and Company, Inc., 1988

Avalanche survival story, pp154–156
Source: Edgar, Luke. '9 Lives: Living to Tell a Backcountry Boarding Story.' http://snowboard.mountainzone.com/2002/story/html/9lives.html, 2002

Capsize survival story, pp171–172
Source: Callahan, Steven. *Adrift: Seventy-six Days Lost at Sea*. Boston: Houghton Mifflin Company, 1986

DIRECTORY OF RESOURCES

The American Meteorological Society (AMS)

http://www.ametsoc.org/AMS
45 Beacon Street
Boston, MA 02108-3693 U.S.A.
Phone: (617) 227-2425
Fax: (617) 742-8718
A nonprofit society for meteorologists and weather enthusiasts. The AMS promotes the development and dissemination of information and education on the atmospheric and related oceanic and hydrologic sciences.

The American Red Cross (ARC)

http://www.redcross.org
National Headquarters
431 18th Street, NW
Washington, DC 20006 U.S.A.
Phone: (202) 639-3520
A volunteer-led humanitarian organization that provides relief to disaster victims and helps to prevent, prepare for, and respond to emergencies.

Atlantic Seasonal Hurricane Activity Forecasts

http://tropical.atmos.colostate.edu
Dr. William M. Gray of the Colorado State University's Department of Atmospheric Science publishes yearly forecasts for tropical storms, named storms, typhoons, hurricanes, and intense hurricanes on this web site. Includes the current forecast and archived forecasts dating back to 1994.

Australian Meteorological and Oceanographic Society (AMOS), Australia

http://www.amos.org.au/Sydney
Melbourne, Victoria 3001, Australia POB 654E
The AMOS is an independent Australian society that supports and fosters interest in meteorology and oceanography through publications, meetings, courses, conferences, grants and prizes. Its site has a weather watch group and links to related resources.

The British Atmospheric Data Centre (BADC)

http://badc.nerc.ac.uk/home
Space Science and Technology Department
R25 Room 2.119
Rutherford Appleton Laboratory
Chilton, Didcot
Oxfordshire, OX11 0QX, U.K.
Phone: 44 (0) 1235 44 64 32
Fax: 44 (0) 1235 44 63 14
The role of this Data Centre (BADC) is to assist UK atmospheric researchers to locate, access and interpret atmospheric data and to ensure the long-term integrity of atmospheric data produced by Natural Environment Research Council (NERC) projects. The BADC has substantial data holdings of its own and also provides information and links to data held by other data centers.

Canadian Meteorological and Oceanographic Society

http://www.cmos.ca
112-150 Louis Pasteur
Ottawa, ON, K1N 6N5 Canada
Phone: (613) 562-5616
Fax: (613) 562-5615
The Society's aim is to promote meteorology and oceanography in Canada. It is a major non-governmental organization serving the interests of meteorologists, climatologists, oceanographers, limnologists, hydrologists and cryospheric scientists in Canada.

The Cooperative Institute for Meteorological Satellite Studies Tropical Cyclone Homepage

http://cimss.ssec.wisc.edu/tropic
Tropical Cyclone Team
University of Wisconsin - Madison
Space Science and Engineering Center
1225 West Dayton Street
Madison, WI 53706 U.S.A.
Provides satellite imagery of active storms and posts Joint Typhoon Warning Center forecasts and National Hurricane Center forecasts on their web site.

European Center for Medium-Range Weather Forecasts (ECMWF), U.K.

http://www.ecmwf.int
Shinfield Park
Reading, Berkshire RG2 9AX, U.K.
Phone: 44 118 949 9000
Fax: 44 118 986 9450

The ECMWF is an international organization supported by twenty-four European States. It provides seasonal, atmosphere global, and ocean wave medium-range weather forecasts.

The Federal Emergency Management Agency (FEMA), U.S.A.

http://www.fema.gov
Federal Emergency Management Agency
Federal Center Plaza
500 C. Street S.W.
Washington, D.C. 20472 U.S.A.

An independent agency of the U.S. federal government with a mission to reduce life and property losses through mitigation and preparedness programs.

Frequently Asked Questions: Hurricanes, Typhoons, and Tropical Cyclones

http://www.aoml.noaa.gov/hrd/tcfaq
Christopher W. Landsea
NOAA AOML/Hurricane Research Division
4301 Rickenbacker Causeway
Miami, Florida 33149 U.S.A.

This web site contains various definitions, answers for some specific questions, and information about the various tropical cyclone basins. It also provides sites that can be accessed for real-time information about tropical cyclones.

The Hurricane Hunters

http://www.hurricanehunters.com

The web site for the 53rd Weather Reconnaissance Squadron, known as the Hurricane Hunters of the U.S. Air Force Reserve. It is the only U.S. Department of Defense organization still flying into tropical storms and hurricanes. This site provides photos of flights inside hurricanes, as well as answers to questions about hurricanes.

Intellicast

http://www.intellicast.com

A service of Weather Services International, this site provides extensive specialized weather information to help plan all outdoor and weather sensitive activities in the U.S.A.

Joint Typhoon Warning Center (JTWC), U.S.A.

http://www.npmoc.navy.mil/jtwc.html

This site is a product of the U. S. Department of Defense agency responsible for issuing tropical cyclone warnings for the Pacific and Indian Oceans.

Meteorological Office, U.K.

http://www.meto.govt.uk
London Road
Bracknell
Berkshire RG12 2SZ, U.K.
Phone: 44 (0)1344 856655
Fax: 44 (0)1344 855681

Public access weather data and forecasts are available on this site, including UK, world and city forecasts, weather warnings, UV index, charts, marine information and satellite imagery.

Meteorological Society of New Zealand

http://metsoc.rsnz.org/index.html
POB 6523
Te Aro, Wellington, New Zealand
Phone: (644) 386 0300
Fax: (644) 386 2153

The Society was inaugurated to encourage an interest in the atmosphere, weather, and climate. This is a group of people from all around New Zealand (and some from overseas) who like sharing their fascination in weather. They publish a quarterly newsletter and biannual journal.

National Climatic Data Center (NCDC), U.S.A.

http://www.ncdc.noaa.gov
Federal Building
151 Patton Avenue
Asheville NC 28801-5001 U.S.A.
Phone: (828) 271-4800
Fax: (828) 271-4876
NCDC provides an historical perspective on climate through the use of over a hundred years of weather observations and the reference databases generated from those observations.

The National Data Buoy Center, U.S.A.

http://www.ndbc.noaa.gov
This web site provides real-time surface weather information over the ocean, as well as archived buoy data.

The National Hurricane Center (NHC), U.S.A.

http://www.nhc.noaa.gov
Tropical Prediction Center
11691 SW 17th Street
Miami, Florida, 33165-2149 U.S.A.
Forecast statements, satellite imagery, historical data, educational material, and reconnaissance reports about hurricanes can all be found here.

National Oceanographic and Atmospheric Administration (NOAA), U.S.A.

http://www.noaa.gov
1305 East-West Highway
8624 Floor
Silver Spring, Maryland 20910 U.S.A.
Phone: (301) 713-1208
NOAA conducts research and gathers data about the global oceans, atmosphere, space, and sun. Its site contains forecasts, weather observations, educational material, and links to NOAA branches.

National Severe Storms Laboratory, U.S.A.

http://www.nssl.noaa.gov
1313 Halley Circle
Norman, Oklahoma 73069 U.S.A.

Phone: (405) 360-3620
Dedicated to improving severe weather warnings and forecasts in order to save lives and reduce property damage, this site provides information on thunderstorms, tornadoes, winter weather, flooding, and damaging winds.

National Weather Service (NWS), U.S.A.

http://www.nws.noaa.gov
US Dept of Commerce
National Oceanic and Atmospheric Administration
National Weather Service
1325 East West Highway
Silver Spring, MD 20910 U.S.A.
NWS provides weather, hydrologic, and climate forecasts and warnings for the United States, its territories, adjacent waters and ocean areas, in order to protect life and property. Warnings, observations, forecasts, and radar imagery can be accessed via this web site.

The Naval Research Laboratory Tropical Cyclone Homepage

http://www.nrlmry.navy.mil/sat-bin/tc_home
Displays satellite imagery of hurricanes and tropical storms around the world.

NOAA Aircraft Operations Center

http://www.aoc.noaa.gov
Aircraft Operations Center (AOC)
P.O. Box 6829
MacDill AFB, FL 33608-0829 U.S.A.
Phone: (813) 828-3310
The airplanes and helicopters of the AOC are equipped with scientific instruments and are flown in support of NOAA's mission to promote global environmental assessment, prediction and stewardship of the Earth's environment. NOAA's aircraft operate throughout the United States and around the world; over open oceans, mountains, coastal wetlands, and Arctic pack ice. This site

provides information on their projects and surveys.

Royal Meteorological Society, U.K.

http://www.royal-met-soc.org.uk
104 Oxford Road
Reading, Berkshire RG1 7LL, U.K.
Phone: 44 0118 956 8500
Fax: 44 0118 956 8571
The Royal Meteorological Society advances and promotes the science of meteorology by means of journals and other publications, discussion meetings, conferences, professional accreditation, grants, medals, prizes, workshops for schoolteachers and other educational activities.

The Tornado Project Online

http://www.tornadoproject.com/index.html
PO Box 302
St. Johnsbury, Vermont 05819 U.S.A.
Gathers, compiles, and makes tornado information available to weather enthusiasts, the meteorological community and emergency management officials. Features of the site include tornado myths, tornado oddities, personal experiences, tornado chasing, tornado safety, and tornadoes in the past as well as more recent tornadoes.

Unisys Weather

http://weather.unisys.com
Comprehensive maps, plots, and satellite data are presented with analyses and forecasts.

Weather Services International, U.K.

http://www.wsi.com
22-24 Vittoria Street
Birmingham, B1 3PU, U.K.
Phone: +44(0) 121 233 7600
Fax: +44(0) 121 233 7666
Recognized as a leading source of weather and weather-related information, WSI serves customers in media, aviation, industry, agri-culture, government, education and consumer markets.

World Meteorological Organization (WMO)

http://www.wmo.ch
7 bis Avenue de la Paix
CP 2300
1211 Geneva 2, Switzerland
Phone: 41 22 730 8111
Fax: 41 22 730 8181
An agency of the United Nations, the WMO handles weather prediction, air pollution research, climate change related activities, ozone layer depletion studies, and tropical storm forecasting. The web site presents official weather forecasts as well as climatological information for selected cities supplied by National Meteorological Services (NMSs) worldwide. Links to their web sites are also provided.